GUERRILLA TACTICS FOR THE GRE™*:

SECRETS AND STRATEGIES THE TEST WRITERS

DON'T WANT YOU TO KNOW

DR. NANCY L. NOLAN

* The GRE is a registered trademark of Educational Testing Services (ETS), which was not involved in the production of, and does not endorse, this publication.

Electronic, CD-ROM, and paperback versions published by:

Magnificent Milestones, Inc.
www.ivyleagueadmission.com

ISBN 978-1-933819-48-8

Disclaimers:

(1) This book was written as a guide; it does not claim to be the definitive word on GRE™ preparation. The opinions expressed are the personal observations of the author based on her own experiences. They are not intended to prejudice any party. Accordingly, the author and publisher do not accept any liability or responsibility for any loss or damage that have been caused, or allegedly caused, through the use of the information in this book.

(2) The GRE is a registered trademark of Educational Testing Services (ETS), which sponsors the test and decides how it will be constructed, administered and used. Neither Dr. Nolan nor Magnificent Milestones, Inc. is affiliated with ETS.

(3) Admission to graduate school depends on several factors in addition to a candidate's GRE™ scores (including GPA, recommendations, interview and essays). The author and publisher cannot guarantee that any applicant will be admitted to any specific school or program if (s)he follows the information in this book.

Dedication

For students everywhere;
may the size of your dreams be exceeded only
by your tenacity to attain them.

Acknowledgements

I am deeply indebted to the students, professors, counselors and admissions officers who have shared their perceptions and frustrations about the GRE™. This book, which was written on your behalf, would not be nearly as powerful without your generous and insightful input.

I also want to thank my colleagues at www.ivyleagueadmission.com for providing a constant source of support, along with the best editorial help in the business.

Guerrilla Tactics for the GRE™ Secrets & Strategies the Test Writers Don't Want You to Know

GUERRILLA TACTICS FOR THE GRE™*:

SECRETS AND STRATEGIES THE TEST WRITERS

DON'T WANT YOU TO KNOW

Chapter 1: Introduction to the GRE™

Few prospects are as frightening to graduate school candidates as the GRE. From an admissions perspective, your concern is not without merit; after years of success in the classroom, your odds of getting into a top-tier program may ultimately hinge on your performance on this marathon, one-day exam. Not surprisingly, an entire cottage industry has evolved to satisfy the increasing demand for books, tapes, CDs and training classes for the GRE. Despite the differences in format and price, the underlying approach for these products is eerily similar; students are advised to read an 800- page book, memorize several thousand vocabulary words and review every math topic known to man.

Sadly, the results of this marathon approach are rarely successful; even worse, it is largely unnecessary. Although the GRE requires an excellent math background and a fairly sophisticated vocabulary, it is a highly *predictable* test that uses the same type of questions (and the same clues and traps) over and over again. For diligent test takers, this predictability offers a great competitive advantage, if you know how to use it.

And that's the difference between *this* book and other GRE guides, which are usually as onerous and intimidating as the exam itself. Although many of them offer helpful suggestions, the typical test taker does not have the time to wade through hours of sample exams (with overly easy "mock" questions), to get to the most usable and practical advice. Far too often, students toss the guides aside after a few hundred pages, without getting the details they need to attain a top score. Inevitably, they walk out of the GRE frustrated and disappointed, wishing there had been a better way to prepare for such a life-changing exam.

Ultimately, that is why we wrote this guide. There IS a better way to conquer the GRE without driving yourself crazy. From our experience, few students have the time to read an 800-page guide before they take the exam; even fewer have the money to complete an expensive test preparation class. For candidates who prefer a shorter, cheaper, and more direct approach to GRE preparation, this guide explains the most important tips and strategies that you need to know to get a top score. We also offer concrete steps to conquer the typical traps and pitfalls that the test takers will inevitably throw your way.

That being said, we absolutely do NOT want to mislead you about your specific chances for success on the GRE. No ethical author or publication can guarantee that a reader will get a perfect score if (s)he follows a particular strategy or approach. Your performance on the GRE will depend, to a certain extent, on factors that are beyond our control, such as your:

1. ability to read and comprehend dense passages quickly and critically
2. overall math and geometry skills
3. extemporaneous writing skills
4. working vocabulary
5. tenacity and stamina on timed exams

Each student bring a unique set of skills and talents to the exam; as a result, GRE questions that are hard for one student may be incredibly easy for another. This is why most one-size-fits-all approaches to GRE preparation are inherently doomed to fail.

And that's why we've taken a different approach in this book, which every test taker can use to his/her advantage. Although we have compiled an impressive amount of information in our appendices (including a review of grammar and math basics and an assortment of vocabulary tools), our goal is NOT to teach you grammar or math. Instead, we are going to teach you the test itself, including the tricks, traps and pitfalls that the GRE writers use to confuse, distract and otherwise deflect your efforts to answer the questions correctly.

Our goal? To help you conquer the GRE, whoever you are, whatever your background, however you choose to prepare for the exam. Like most battles, preparation and skills are only half the equation. The other half is knowing your target, warts and all, before you enter the battlefield.

The Nature of the Beast

The GRE is a 2- hour and 30- minute exam that is designed to test your reading, writing and mathematical skills. The exam is divided into three sections - Verbal, Quantitative and Analytical Writing. Except for the writing section, which requires students to write two original essays, the questions are primarily in multiple-choice format (students must select the correct answer from five possibilities).

The **Verbal Section** of the GRE includes 30 multiple choice questions, which are presented in one 30-minute segment. They will include:

6 Sentence Completion questions
7 Analogy questions
9 Antonym questions
8 Reading Comprehension questions

The **Quantitative Section** of the GRE includes 28 questions, which are presented in one 45-minute section. They will include:

14 Quantitative Comparison questions
10 Mathematical Word Problems
4 Data Interpretation questions

The **Analytical Writing Section** of the GRE includes 2 essay prompts, which require students to write two original essays within 75-minutes. They will include:

Perspective on an Issue
Analysis of an Argument

The GRE also includes an experimental section, in which the writers will test new questions for future editions of the exam. This section will not count toward your score. Unfortunately, you will not know which section of the GRE is experimental when you take the exam, because it will look the same as the other sections. Consequently, you should never try to guess which section is experimental; tackle *every* section with the expectation that it will count.

For the Verbal and Quantitative sections, of the GRE, you will earn individual scores between 200 and 800, which will be added together to give you an overall GRE score between 400 and 1600. For the Analytical Writing Section, you will receive a score between 1 and 6.

A Word on Tips, Secrets and Strategies

At this point, you may be wondering what is so unique or special about this publication. After all, every GRE book gives readers a list of tips or strategies. Our first "inside secret" is that the entire list of tips in most books, albeit informative, doesn't begin to scratch the surface of what you need to know (and do) to ace this exam. Most "hot tips and strategies" are really just obvious, common sense things that all students should do before they walk in the door on the day of the test.

In actuality, getting a top score on the GRE hinges on TWO factors:

a. Knowing the material that the exam tests
b. Knowing the tricks of the test writers, who tend to ask the *same* types of questions, with the *same* types of trips, traps and pitfalls, the *same* way on every exam

As a student, you spent years in school to master the material that is tested on the GRE. In contrast, you can learn the tricks of the test writers (and develop a plan to tackle them), in just a few days. From our perspective, it is an essential step in GRE preparation.

Why are we publishing this information? Because we think that all students deserve a level playing field for the GRE, which requires an appreciation of not only WHAT you will be asked, but HOW you will be asked. As authors, we can't control where you went to school or how well you did in your math and English classes. Your mastery of these topics will undoubtedly have a major impact on your subsequent GRE scores. What we CAN provide is guidance and insight into how the test questions are asked, and the best ways to approach them. We will also reveal the topics, problems and ideas that are tested over and over again, without fail, on *every* GRE.

Most test preparation books have a vague goal of "helping" the reader get a higher score on the GRE. Our goal is much more ambitious than that; we want to open your mind to the *predictability* of this test, which makes it inherently *learnable*. And learning this test is as important to your eventual score as learning English, writing or math. When armed with the appropriate information, you will undoubtedly discover that the "GRE monster" isn't nearly as formidable as you had feared.

Before we begin, here is our own obligatory list of common sense things to do before you take the GRE:

1) Be familiar with the types of questions in each section and the underlying material they will cover. Refresh your skills in basic grammar and mathematics until you are 100% comfortable with each idea or concept.

2) Know how long you have to complete each section and pace yourself accordingly. A general rule of thumb for the GRE: each question that you answer correctly adds 10 points to your score. It doesn't matter whether you earn your points from the easy questions or the hard ones; you simply want to answer as many questions correctly in the time allotted.

3) Don't waste time reading the instructions on the day of the test. We include the specific instructions for each question type in this publication. Read them thoroughly and make sure you understand them. This will save you several minutes on the actual day of the test.

4) Develop a strategy to attack the questions in each section according to their level of difficulty. Remember, each question is worth one point, regardless of whether it is easy or hard. Learn to recognize (and seek out) the types of questions that you are good at. Answer as many "easy" ones first; leave the more challenging, time-consuming questions until the end.

5) Answer every question, even if you are clueless about how to approach it. In many cases, you are better off guessing than wasting a ton of time on a question or problem that you aren't able to solve. The GRE questions will vary widely in their level of difficulty. Further, each student brings a unique set of strengths and skills to the exam, which will influence his/her performance. Some questions are designed to be extremely difficult for all students. On such a rigidly timed test, they should not consume a disproportionate amount of your time.

6) Use your knowledge of the GRE scoring policies to develop an optimal guessing strategy. For all sections except Reading Comprehension (in which the questions are presented in random order), GRE questions are presented in the order of difficulty. The test writers will ask the "easy" ones first, followed by the ones that they consider to be "harder." Since all questions are worth the same, you should slow down and focus most of your time on the first (easiest) ones. Make sure you get as many of the "easy" points as possible before you tackle the more difficult questions.

On the GRE, you will receive 1 point for every correct answer and 0 points for every answer you leave blank (or answer incorrectly). On a practical level, this means that there is *no penalty for guessing*. Consequently, you should guess the answer to any question if you can eliminate just ONE answer choice.

7) Keep track of time as you work on each section of the test. Although we will teach you many strategies for different types of questions, you must work quickly and efficiently to apply them to as many questions as possible.

8) Be extremely careful with your answer grid. Make sure you record your answers properly and skip spaces properly if you jump around during the test. We recommend that you circle the correct answer to each question in your test booklet, in addition to recording it on your answer grid. Circle questions that you are skipping, so that you can find them easily later when you return to them. Take a minute at the end of each section to verify that you have recorded your all of your answers onto your answer grid properly.

9) Don't try to cram a lot of studying into the last few days before the test. Your best bet is to prepare a few hours per day for several weeks before the exam and to relax (or try to relax) the day or so before the actual test.

10) Arrive at the test center a few minutes early with all of your essential supplies (photo ID card, admission ticket, sharpened #2 pencils, watch, comfortable clothing and healthy snack). Avoid chatting about the test during the breaks; this nervous chatter usually just increases self-doubt and anxiety.

11) For many students, the GRE is very different from any other test they have ever taken. It's extremely long. It contains ridiculously difficult words. And there's no credit for "showing your work" or getting a question "half right." All that matters is whether or not you fill in the correct letters on the answer grid.

As a result, many students walk away feeling like they "blew it," when they actually did quite well. In a panic, they cancel their scores. We strongly discourage you from doing this. From our experience, few students have a realistic perspective of how they actually did on the test. Many times, their bad feelings are simply a culmination of the stress that accompanies such a long, hard exam. Don't panic and cancel your score unless:

a) You were seriously ill on the test day (and it affected your performance)
b) You were woefully unprepared (and plan to remedy that before taking the test again)

12) Give careful thought to the format in which you take the test. In many locations, you will be offered the choice of taking the computerized version (CAT) of the GRE, rather than the paper-based version. From our perspective, you should DEFINITELY avoid the computerized version of this exam!

Why? On the GRE-CAT, you must answer the questions in the order in which they are asked. You cannot skip questions and return to them later; you also cannot change your answer to a question once you submit it. Most importantly, you cannot seek out and answer the *easiest questions first*, which is a critical strategy on most sections of the GRE.

Over the years, we have coached dozens of students for the GRE. Without exception, they have ALL fared better on the paper version of the test, which allows them to better manage their time. Although it lacks the "sexiness" and sophistication of the high tech option, it offers the best chance to employ the strategies in this publication to ensure the best possible score. To us, it's well worth the inconvenience.

13) Students frequently ask us whether or not they will benefit from a formal test prep class or one-on-one tutoring. To be honest, it depends on whether or not you are organized and motivated. When we surveyed students about their test prep experiences (including graduates of our own course), they cited the following benefits as being most important to them:

1. Practicing with actual test questions
2. Taking mock exams under the same time constraints as the GRE
3. Developing their own personalized strategy for each section of the exam

A test prep class forces students to accomplish these tasks in a classroom setting. No doubt about it; this reinforcement of the exam topics, along with the format and style of the actual test, can give students a definite edge. Nevertheless, if you are highly motivated, you can easily accomplish the same goals by working with sample tests and review materials at home. Many students who achieve top scorers on the GRE do so by working with publications like this one on their own schedule (and initiative).

From our perspective, the only students who MUST attend a special class (or hire a tutor) are those who have serious deficiencies in the areas that the GRE tests. If you failed algebra and never took geometry, you would obviously not be well positioned to succeed on the quantitative portion of the exam. In that situation, you should either delay the GRE until you could complete those classes or hire a tutor to explain the basic concepts to you.

How to Use this Publication

By design, we have divided our course on GRE preparation into separate publications, to give you a targeted approach to suit your specific needs. **This** publication literally "teaches the test;" it presents relevant strategies for each section of the GRE. Although we include 100 pages of useful background material in the Appendices, our goal is not to teach you the underlying math or English concepts that will be covered.

For students who desire a comprehensive review of ALL topics that are tested on the GRE, including 1000 realistic practice questions (and solutions), we are proud to offer *Guerrilla Review for the GRE: 1,001 Practice Questions & Answers* (ISBN: 978-1-933819-42-6) . Use this publication to boost your skills in the most critical areas and to build your confidence with difficult question types.

For students who need additional practice for the quantitative section of the exam, *Killer Math Word Problems for Standardized Tests (SAT, GRE, GMAT): When Plugging Numbers into Formulas Just Isn't Enough* (ISBN: 978-1-933819-46-4) offers a complete review of the thirty types of word problems you are likely to see, including 600 sample problems. Learn how to answer these questions quickly and accurately on the day of the test.

Finally, for students who are comfortable with the concepts on the GRE and **really** want to challenge themselves before the big day, we are delighted to offer *The Toughest GRE Practice Test We've Ever Seen* (ISBN: 978-1-933819-45-7). Use this publication – and complete the mock exam - AFTER you have completed your preparation program. See how your performance compares to those of other highly competitive students.

Now, let's dissect the GRE.

Chapter 2: Vocabulary Tips for the GRE™

The Verbal section of the GRE will test your vocabulary in a number of ways:

Antonym questions, in which you will be asked to identify the answer choice that means the *opposite* of a specific word or phrase

Analogy questions, which present two words that are related to each other. Among the five answer choices, you must identify another pair of words that are related in the same way

Sentence completion questions, which require you to select the correct word to complete a logical sentence or thought

Reading comprehension questions, which will ask you to define or explain the meaning of a word in a particular context

To no one's surprise, all of these sections are laced with difficult words that students must know to answer the questions correctly. Fortunately, the test writers continue to use several fairly predictable tricks and traps when they write these questions. By anticipating (and preparing for) them, savvy students can ace these sections of the exam WITHOUT memorizing the definitions of thousands of unfamiliar words.

In fact, from our perspective, most test prep classes take an overly ambitious approach to vocabulary that we feel is inherently misguided. Without exception, they present students with a list of 3,000 to 5,000 definitions to memorize in the weeks before the test. The problem is, most students must balance their GRE preparation with their college courses, outside jobs and numerous personal responsibilities. Few of them have the time or energy to retain thousands of new definitions for the big day. In fact, we know several students who became overwhelmed by the lists that they began to confuse the words. On the actual exam, they easily fell into one of the test writers' main traps.

Let's be honest about the vocabulary challenges of the GRE; unless you have a crystal ball, there is no way you will know exactly what words will appear on the exam. Whether you memorize 300 words or 3,000, there's an excellent chance that at least one or two words will appear that you don't know. The solution, however, is NOT to memorize more words, but to focus your attention on those what are **most likely** to show up on the GRE. By focusing on the test writers' most popular tricks and traps, you can achieve excellent results with far less preparation time.

In this chapter, we will describe the resources that are included in the Appendices, along with our detailed strategies for using them:

Appendix 1. Learning Words by their Prefixes, Roots & Suffixes
Appendix 2. Practical Groupings of the GRE's Most Commonly Tested Words
Appendix 3. Tricky Look-alike (and Sound-alike) Words
Appendix 4. 200 Commonly Tested Words (in Context)

Strategy 1. Our first strategy, unfortunately, is the driest and most boring one. Since the English language is derived primarily from Latin and Greek words, an efficient (general) approach to building your vocabulary is to study a list of the most common prefixes, roots and suffixes that are used (Appendix 1). Study the lists at your leisure, noting the many practical examples that we have provided for each term. Then, as you continue to prepare for the test, note the many occasions in which you can use your knowledge of roots and suffixes to decipher the meaning of a new word.

Example 1. AMICABLE

Let's assume that you don't know what the word amicable means. From studying the list of roots and suffixes, you could figure it out by breaking the word into its individual parts.

The prefix "ami" means love
The suffix "able" means capable of

Thus, we can reasonably conclude that amicable means capable of love.

Example 2. HYPOTHERMIA

The term "hypo" means under, while "therm" means heat." Finally, the suffix "ia" means disease.

From this information, we can correctly determine that hypothermia is a medical condition in which the body temperature is too low.

Although this is a terrific technique to build your vocabulary, few students like it. Unfortunately, even fewer have the patience to memorize a long list of roots and suffixes, with no guarantee that their efforts will pay off on the day of the exam. Over the years, we've been asked a million times if there is a better way to conquer the vocabulary section on the GRE. I'm thrilled to say, "Absolutely!" Read on.

Strategy 2. Many students are stunned to discover that they only need to know the *general meaning* of words (rather than exact definitions) for the Analogy, Antonym, and Sentence Completion questions on the GRE. They are even MORE stunned to learn that the test writers tend to limit their questions to the same 15 to 20 *groups of words*…… and their *opposites*. This is definitely a situation that savvy students can use to their advantage. If you study sample GREs, you will notice several similarities in Sentence Completion questions:

1. Most of the sentences are written in a similar manner; the blank(s) are *adjectives* that describe a person, mood, place or situation.

2. The clues in the sentence indicate the tone of the word, along with its intensity.

3. With rare exceptions, the test writers focus on the same 20 or 30 word meanings:

Old or new
Happy or sad
Rich or poor
Proud or humble
Courageous or timid
Generous or cheap
To praise someone or insult them
To calm someone or make the situation worse
Pleasant and unpleasant personality traits

4. Further, the four incorrect answer choices nearly ALWAYS include a difficult or unusual word that means exactly the **opposite** of the correct word! If the student has not followed the logic of the question, or, in questions with two blanks, has misinterpreted the relationship between the two words, these "opposites" represent a classic (and avoidable) trap.

Appendix 2 offers a valuable list of frequently tested words grouped according to their general meaning. Directly after each group, we have included a similar group of words that mean exactly the *opposite*. Read through the groupings carefully, noting that the words in each group are not perfect synonyms, but similar enough to work in Sentence Completion questions. Also note the words that mean the *opposite* of those words. As we've said, they are wildly popular answer choices with the test writers.

Example 1. Jenny had a tendency to be _____ with her friends, always loaning them money and buying them expensive gifts.

     a.   parsimonious
     b.   cogent
     c.   munificent
     d.   capricious
     e.   mendicant

In this case, we are looking for a word that means generous or benevolent. The correct choice is answer C, munificent.

If you did not know the correct answer, note how helpful the information in Appendix 2 would have been. Below, I have copied the two lists of words from that Appendix that mean generous and cheap. Not only was the correct answer choice on the list; one of the words that means the *opposite* of generous was also included as an incorrect answer choice as a trap.

Generous: Altruistic, beneficent, benevolent, charitable, effusive, humanitarian, magnanimous, <u>munificent</u>, philanthropic

Cheap: Frugal, miserly, paltry, <u>parsimonious</u>, penurious, provident, thrifty

Although the 10 words listed under "generous" differ slightly in meaning, the GRE rarely explores such minor differences. Its focus, inevitably, is whether or not students can distinguish the words on one of the lists from those on the other.

Example 2. Jane's _____ attitude at work was particularly impressive, considering her recent painful injury.

> a. nascent
> b. assiduous
> c. indolent
> d. ethereal
> e. timorous

Here, we are seeking a positive word that relates to good performance in the workplace. In Appendix 2, you will find the word "assiduous," which is the correct answer, under the heading "hard working." Likewise, the list of words with the opposite meaning (lazy) includes one of the incorrect answer choices as a trap.

Hard Working: <u>Assiduous</u>, diligent, persevering, tenacious

Lazy: Apathetic, <u>indolent</u>, insipid, languid, lethargic, torpor,

Example 3. Although she was proud of her many accomplishments, Rachel remained _____ when she was offered praise.

> a. turgid
> b. mercurial
> c. mendicant
> d. impudent
> e. demure

The correct answer is a word that means humble or unassuming. Choice E (demure) is the best answer. Not surprisingly, the test writers also included impudent, a word that means the opposite of humble. For students who studied the groups of words in Appendix 2, and were able to classify them correctly (see lists below), this question was fairly easy.

Humble: <u>Demure</u>, diffident, indisposed, laconic, plebian, reticent, subdued, subservient, taciturn, timorous, unassuming, unpretentious, unostentatious

Overly Proud: Affected, arrogant, aristocratic, audacious, authoritarian, condescending, disdainful, despotic, egotistical, flippant, haughty, imperious, <u>impudent</u>, insolent, ostentatious, patronizing, pompous, supercilious, superiority, vainglorious

In recent test preparation classes, we have received incredibly positive feedback from students on our list of word groupings in Appendix 2. If learning them in this manner is a good fit for your personal learning style, then by all means do so. We are sure that the technique will help you to earn several points on the GRE. If not, read on for another strategy that will inevitably come in handy on the verbal portion of the exam.

Strategy 3. Students with limited vocabularies – and non-native speakers of English - are blind to the many words in our language that look and sound alike, but have dramatically different meanings, such as:

Adulate and adulterate
Antipathy and apathy
Ascetic, aseptic and aesthetic
Commensurate and commiserate
Discreet and discrete
Explicate and extricate
Heterogeneous and homogeneous
Illicit and elicit
Ingenious and ingenuous
Waver and waiver
Exacerbate, exonerate and exculpate
Fervid and florid
Prodigal and prodigious

As you probably suspect, the test writers LOVE to include tricky look-alike words as incorrect answer choices on the GRE. In fact, I've rarely seen a copy of the exam that did NOT include at least one or two words from Appendix 3, which provides a list of the most commonly confused words (and their meanings).

From our perspective, no one should walk into the test without reviewing this list at least once. The words will help you to navigate not only the Sentence Completion questions, but the Reading Comprehension questions (and answer choices as well).

Example. Like her sister, who was extremely cautious, Jane was a _____ young woman.

    a.   munificent
    b.   prudent
    c.   discrete
    d.   indolent
    e.   dauntless

The correct answer is a synonym of cautious, which is prudent, answer choice B. However, the test writers have cleverly tried to confuse the issue by including the word *discrete* as an answer choice, which looks and sounds like *discreet*, another synonym for cautious and prudent. For students who do not know the difference in meanings (and spellings), this is a classic trap.

Strategy 4. For students who prefer to learn words in context, we have also included a list of 200 commonly tested words as they are used in regular conversation (Appendix 4). For words that you already know, this is a great way to reinforce their meanings. For words you do not know, we encourage you to build your OWN sentences, in which you relate the word to someone (or something) you know.

Example 1: The word *alleviate* means "to make more bearable." If your father is a physician, a terrific (and memorable) sentence would be, "Patients request medication from Dad to alleviate their pain."

Example 2: The word *dilatory* means "intended to delay." If your best friend is putting off studying for the GRE, a useful sentence might be, "Julie employed several dilatory means to avoid studying for the test."

The sentences are short (and possibly silly), but you are far more likely to remember them than something generic. In fact, that's how most people learn new words: from the context in which they are used. Once the reader is confident of the word's meaning, (s)he will use it to describe the people, places and situations in his/her own life.

As you read through our many Appendices, you may struggle to remember (or distinguish) different words. For the most difficult ones, if you take the time to write a sentence and use the word in the correct context, you are FAR more likely to use the word again (and remember it on the day of the test).

No doubt about it - it's boring. And tedious. And probably the last thing you want to do on a warm Sunday afternoon, But repetition works well when you are trying to build your vocabulary, which is why we recommend it so strongly.

Strategy 5. This next strategy is helpful, but not foolproof. When you learn new words on the lists we provide, note how often the words with positive meanings **sound** positive. Likewise, many words that are negative sound as nasty as their meanings.

Example: Prefixes and roots that mean "good" have positive sounds, such as peri, bene, omni, magni, pro and vita. In your daily life, you use words with these roots, such as benevolent, omniscient and vitamin, which are positive in nature.

Likewise, roots such as mal, anti and dis remind us of the negative words which are derived from them, including malignant, antiestablishment and disrespectful.

This isn't a foolproof technique, though, because many words that mean "not" and "un" will be positive, if they mean the opposite of a negative, such as antibiotic and anti-venom. But the concept is worthwhile for many students, who already have a working use of many roots and prefixes.

Strategy 6. From our experience, most students have better vocabulary skills than they realize. Unfortunately, when they sit down for the GRE, they become nervous and overwhelmed, which diminishes their ability to approach the question calmly and logically.

Don't psyche yourself out on the GRE. Ultimately, that is the biggest trap of all. Instead, approach vocabulary challenges strategically. When you encounter a word on the test that you don't know, stay calm. Try to identify the root or prefix. If you can recognize even a *single part* of the word (such as ami in amicable, ant in antonym or grad in gradient), you can often infer its correct meaning.

If you can't identify a recognizable root or suffix, see if it is one of the commonly tested words in Appendices 2 through 4. Is it a tricky look-alike word? The opposite of a word you know? Use every possible clue to deduce its meaning.

Finally, if you draw a complete blank, try to determine the word's meaning from the context in which it is used. Plug the answer choice into the sentence and see if it sounds right. You've been speaking and writing English for many years. By doing so, you have cultivated a good feel for what "sounds" right and what doesn't. Go with your gut. When it comes to vocabulary, you will undoubtedly find that you know far more words than you think you do.

Chapter 3: Sentence Completion Questions

The GRE includes 6 Sentence Completion questions, in which one (or two) words in each statement are intentionally left blank. Students must choose the correct word(s) for the blank(s) from the five answer choices provided.

The Sentence Completion section is designed to assess:

1. the extent of your vocabulary
2. your logical understanding of the overall sentence

Here are the specific instructions on the test:

Directions*: For each question in this section, select the best answer from among the choices given and fill the corresponding circle on the answer sheet.*

Like many sections of the GRE, Sentence Completion questions are presented in the order of difficulty; the "easy" ones are first, followed by those that are "harder." Since all questions are worth the same, you should slow down and focus most of your time on the first (easiest) questions. Make sure you get as many of the "easy" points as possible before you invest time in the more difficult questions.

For many students, the Sentence Completion section of the GRE is one of the easiest parts of the exam. Nevertheless, the questions contain several traps and pitfalls that savvy students should avoid.

Strategy 1. Thankfully, Sentence Completion questions are never vague; each will include an adjective or descriptive phrase that will indicate the meaning of the missing word. Your first step in tackling a question is to read the statement in its entirety and decide (*without* looking at the answer choices) what word would best complete the sentence. Then, and ONLY then, should you look at the five choices and try to choose among them.

Some Sentence Completion questions will be so easy that you will determine the meaning of the missing word without much effort. The more difficult questions, however, will require a more sophisticated approach. When you read each sentence, look for key words that indicate what is happening. These key words will tell you whether the missing word is:

a. positive or negative
b. a synonym or antonym of another word in the sentence

The GRE writers use three groups of key words as **clues** in Sentence Completion questions:

1. Words that indicate the same direction. In this situation, the second phrase supports the first:

And, also, in addition, additionally, too, or, besides, moreover, furthermore, therefore and in fact.

Note: The test writers may also use a colon (:) or a semi-colon (;) for the same purpose, which is to indicate that the next phrase supports, explains or amplifies the first.

2. Words that indicate a different direction. In this situation, the second phrase disputes or contrasts with the first:

But, ironically, nevertheless, however, instead, yet, despite, in spite of, nonetheless, unless, although, not, except, while, rather, on the other hand

3. Words that suggest cause and effect. In this case, the second phrase not only amplifies the first, but indicates that one situation caused the other:

17

Because, therefore, as a result, consequently, since, so, by, accordingly, when

Example 1. Although Rick is a wealthy man, he is notorious for his _____ ways.

The word *although* indicates a contrast. Another clue in the sentence is the word *notorious*, which means famous in a negative way. Therefore, we can conclude that the missing word means the opposite of generous. The correct answer choice would be a synonym for cheap or tight-fisted. From our list in Appendix 2, possible answers are frugal, miserly, parsimonious, penurious or thrifty.

Example 2. Michael tended to be argumentative in class; moreover, his condescending tone tended to _____ his classmates.

The semi-colon in this sentence, along with the word *moreover*, indicates that the second clause will amplify the first. Another clue is the word *condescending*, which describes the negative attitude to which Michael's classmates are responding. Our missing word, therefore, must be a synonym for alienate, put off or insult.

Example 3. Because medicine is a _____ profession, many students enroll in pre-medical courses with dollar signs in their eyes.

The word *because* indicates both support and explanation. Hence, we know that the second part of the sentence will follow the same direction as the first part. The second clue is *dollar signs*, which tells us that the missing word is a synonym for lucrative or well-paying.

Strategy 2. As we noted in Chapter 2, the GRE writers tend to be fairly predictable in the types of words that they use in this section of the exam, You must not only master these vocabulary words, but be prepared for the tricks and traps that the writers will place in your path.

Apply the strategies in Chapter 2 to learn the most commonly tested words on this section of the GRE. Study Appendices 1 through 4 until you feel comfortable with as many new words as possible. Pay particular attention to the list of tricky look-alike words (Appendix 3) and to the list of word groupings (Appendix 2) that the test writers tend to favor. Also review the strategies in Chapter 2 that demonstrate how the test writers try to trick students by providing antonyms and look-alike words as possible answer choices. From our perspective, these traps are so prevalent that they warrant additional examples.

Example 1. Despite Julie's ebullience in the classroom, she was often _____ in social situations.

     a.   melancholy
     b.   condescending
     c.   scintillating
     d.   innovative
     e.   philosophical

In this sentence, we are looking for a word that means the opposite of ebullient (lively and excited). Acceptable words would be any terms that convey shyness or social awkwardness. The correct answer choice is A, *melancholy*. A trap in the answer choices is C, scintillating, which is similar in meaning as ebullient, and the *opposite* of the correct answer. The GRE writers LOVE to set this trap.

Example 2. Unlike other students, who took a familiar approach to the problem, Janet's solution was _____ and clever.

     a.   hackneyed
     b.   ingenuous
     c.   ambiguous
     d.   original
     e.   immutable

Here, the correct answer is a word that means original or innovative. Hence, choice D (*original*) is correct. In this question, however, the test writers have included a trap in answer choice B for unsuspecting students. The word *ingenuous* looks and sounds a lot like *ingenious*, which is a synonym for the correct answer choice. Ingenuous and ingenious are tricky look-alike words that have different meanings. When you see one of them on the GRE, be on the alert for clever test writing traps.

Strategy 3. A common ploy of the writers is to include answer choices that relate to the *topic* of the sentence, but are an incorrect match for the missing word. For example, a sentence about the law might include answer choices such as litigate and arbitrate, while a sentence about religion will include answer choices such as sacrosanct and consecrate. Don't be blinded (or misguided) by terminology that relates to a particular topic or field. By design, the GRE is general in scope; it is purposely written to eliminate biases in favor of one particular subject area. As a result, the correct answer to a Sentence Completion question will rarely be a word that is only used by one profession.

To avoid this trap, focus strictly on the meaning of the missing word. Don't be distracted by the topic of the sentence itself.

Example. The Senator's desire to impress her constituents, not her commitment to Hurricane Katrina victims, was the impetus for her _____ disaster recovery referendum.

     a.   autocratic
     b.   assiduous
     c.   dogmatic
     d.   provident
     e.   effusive

The correct answer is a word that means generous, which is answer choice E, *effusive*. A potential trap is answer choice D, *provident*, which means the opposite of generous. Another possible pitfall is the word *autocratic*, which refers to a government in which one person has complete power. Although this question is about a government official (and a referendum), the word autocratic is NOT the best answer choice. It is a trap for students who focus on the topic of the sentence, rather than the meaning of the missing word.

Strategy 4. When evaluating answer choices, keep in mind the tone of the sentence and the level of emotion that the missing word must convey. A common ploy of the writers is to include an answer choice that is perfectly reasonable when you test it in the sentence, but does not capture the tone of the sentence properly. The *best* answer choice will not overstate or understate the underlying emotion, but be an exact fit for the situation. Be alert to these "shades of gray," which are particularly significant in the harder (later) questions in the section.

Example: To _____ the irate man whose flight was cancelled, the gate agent offered a complimentary dinner and hotel room.

     a.   excoriate
     b.   mediate
     c.   acknowledge
     d.   placate
     e.   solicit

In this sentence, the missing word is a verb that means to satisfy, appease or compensate. The correct answer is D, or *placate*.

When we review the list of answer choices, there are **two** potentials traps for students to avoid. The first is the word *excoriate*, which is answer choice A. Excoriate means *to criticize*, which is obviously not the correct answer. Unfortunately, the word *excoriate* looks and sounds a lot like the word *expiate*, which DOES have the correct meaning as our answer choice. Students who are rushing or confused might select *excoriate* by mistake, thinking that it is *expiate*. By doing so, they would get the question wrong.

The second trap is the word *acknowledge*, which is answer choice C. Although the word "works" in the blank, it is not the BEST of the five answer choices, because it doesn't go far enough. The gate agent not only acknowledged the man's complaint, but rectified it. Hence, the word *placate*, which means to soothe by making concessions, is a better choice.

Strategy 5. Over the years, the GRE writers have learned how to exploit the students' tendency to memorize roots and prefixes. In Sentence Completion questions, look for tricky answers whose root or prefix matches the subject or tone of the sentence, but are the incorrect answer choice.

<u>Example</u>: When she realized the _____ of her mistake, Sandra became humble and apologetic.

    a.   insouciance
    b.   gravure
    c.   reticence
    d.   enormity
    e.   prudence

In this sentence, the correct word would be a synonym for magnitude, gravity, significance, or enormity. Hence, answer choice D, *enormity*, is correct. Choice B is a trick for students who know that the root "grav" means heavy or significant. Unfortunately, look-alike word *gravure* is a type of printing process; its meaning has nothing to do with the root. The other answer choices are also traps, because they are synonyms and antonyms of other words in the sentence, such as humble and apologetic, which *explain* the situation, but do not match the meaning of the missing word.

Strategy 6. If you do not know the answer to a Sentence Completion question, use common sense to eliminate incorrect answer choices. First, eliminate words that are not grammatically correct. Next, eliminate words that are the wrong type (you need a noun and one of the choices is an adjective). Third, eliminate any choices that are not the right "direction" (you need a word than means generous, and the answer choice means boisterous).

Once you take these steps, you will probably have narrowed your choices to two or three possibilities. Quickly plug them into the original sentence and read it back. See if it makes sense. On tough questions, it's easy to get confused and pick a positive word when you need a negative one. Don't lose points because of carelessness. Additionally, you can often eliminate one or two answer choices when you read them back in context, simply because they don't "sound right." Trust your ear.

Finally, if you are confronted with two possible answer choices that both seem to fit, try to identify the difference between the two words. One answer will always fit better than the other. Your job is to identify the BEST choice, by determining the most specific word that doesn't overstate or understate the emotion or tone of the sentence. The harder the questions, the more your decisions will likely hinge on this type of subtlety.

Strategy 7. For Sentence Completion questions with two blanks, determine the **relationship** between the two missing words. Are they both positive? Is one positive and the other negative? Are they synonyms or antonyms of each other?

Once you know the *relationship* between the two words, use it to select the correct answer choice. First, eliminate answers in which one (or both) words are not going in the right direction. Then, eliminate answer choices in which the first choice is correct, but not the second one. In these situations, the writers are testing whether or not you "caught" the direction in which the sentence was going. (If you are rushing, you might fall into this trap and not even know it.)

<u>Example</u>: After an extensive search for a new Corporate Treasurer, the selection committee's choice won the immediate _____ of the managers, although a few of them had _____ about her.

    a.   skepticism….apprehension
    b.   acclaim….reservations
    c.   ire…preconceptions
    d.   disapproval…repercussions
    e.   approval…..disagreements

In this sentence, the word *won* tells us that the first word is positive. Likewise, the word *although* indicates that the second word is negative.

When we review the answer choices, we can immediately eliminate choices A, C, and D, because the first word is not positive. This leaves us with choices B and E. Upon further inspection, we can eliminate choice E, because it makes no sense. (If the managers approved of her, why would they have disagreements?) When we read back answer choice B, which is the correct answer, it makes perfect sense. The managers approved of the candidate, but a few had reservations about her.

Strategy 8. In sentences with two missing words, don't be intimidated by odd or unusual answer choices. In most cases, you will usually know the meaning of at least one of the two words. Work with the easier blank first. Often, you can eliminate one or two answer choices simply because the "easy" word in the pair doesn't fit.

Example: When the FBI investigated the fraud at Enron, they made a startling discovery; some of the formulas to over-inflate earnings required such _____ strategies that only the most _____ agents could decipher them.

      a.   onerous…nefarious
      b.   extraneous…. decorous
      c.   intricate…adroit
      d.   amorphous…calumniate
      e.   anachronistic…extrapolate

Because of the big words in the answer choices, many students would be intimidated. Don't fall for the smoke and mirrors. The sentence provides plenty of key words that indicate that the first missing word is a negative one that describes the fraudulent strategies to overstate earnings at Enron. We can also conclude that the second missing word describes the type of agent who could understand (and decipher) these strategies.

The answer choices contain a number of odd and unusual words. Don't let this deter you; simply apply the strategies and eliminate incorrect answers. Even if you can't eliminate anything, plug the five pairs into the blanks and read the sentences back. The *correct* answer, choice C, is perfectly understandable. The test writers simply buried it in the middle of several odd combinations of rarely used words. None of the other combinations makes a bit of sense.

If you complete every Sentence Correction question on the GRE, you will likely encounter at least one of these over-written, aimed-to-confuse questions. Stay calm. Apply the strategies we have presented here. You can conquer the GRE monster!

Strategy 9. Be prepared for questions in which the missing words do not go in the direction that you expect. On higher level questions, which are significantly more difficult than the earlier ones, the test writers have been known to throw a few curveballs.

Example: Only an authority in mathematics could _____ the _____ subject matter that the Nobel Prize winner discussed.

      a.   attenuate….esoteric
      b.   portent….intricate
      c.   condone….ambiguous
      d.   reproduce….heretical
      e.   debunk….fabricated

In this question, the only key words are *authority in mathematics* and *Nobel Prize winner*. Further, there are no words that indicate a contrast, which leads us to believe that both words will go in the same direction. At first blush, the topic of the sentence seems to indicate that the words *must* be positive. After all, this is a Nobel Prize winner we are talking about.

Look again. There is nothing in this sentence that indicates tone, which means that **any** set of answer choices in which the words go in the same direction is fair game. Students who immediately assume that the first word HAS to be positive would eliminate answer choice E, which is the correct answer. Once they did, they would find themselves with answer choices that made little or no sense.

Why are we presenting an example that is an exception to the rules? For two reasons:

(1) the test writers are notorious for creating them. We want you to be prepared.
(2) it demonstrates the importance of applying Strategy 6 when all else fails.

If you drew a blank on this one, Strategy 6 suggests that you plug all of the answer choices into the sentence and read it through. When you do, you are forced to look at the sentence in a whole new way, in which answer choice E immediately falls into place. If the work being discussed was not authentic (i.e., fabricated), then only an authority in mathematics could prove it (i.e., debunk it). It is a surprising question, and somewhat unusual, but not unprecedented on the GRE.

Strategy 10. By design, the toughest questions (and vocabulary words) will be presented in the last few Sentence Completion questions. This is where you are most likely to encounter a question in which the answer choices are words that you don't know, such as little-used monsters like calumny, truculence and apocryphal.

Over the years, we've discovered a fascinating trend on these tough questions. Many students, after they employ all of our strategies, are able to narrow down their answer choices to two words; one that almost fits the sentence (but not quite) and one that they do not know. *In 90% of these situations, you should choose the word that you don't know, rather than the one that doesn't seem like a good fit.*

Why? At the end of a section, the writers know you will be tired and confused. They also know that you will be intimidated by the three-dollar word and afraid to choose it. In effect, they are COUNTING on you to choose an answer choice that "sort of" fits, just because you are comfortable with the word's meaning. Sadly, most students fall right into this trap.

Don't be intimidated by words that you don't know. If you can realistically eliminate the other four answer choices, you must be confident enough choose the one that is left. Don't settle for an answer that isn't right just because you can pronounce it.

Strategy 11. Now that you've learned the Sentence Completion strategies, try your hand at some sample questions. The answers are presented at the end of this chapter.

1. Only a _____ could have anticipated the unusual combination of life-changing events that occurred that fateful day.

     a.   engineer
     b.   humanitarian
     c.   clairvoyant
     d.   philanthropist
     e.   statistician

2. Claire attributed her strong sense of _____ to her parents, who encouraged her to give back to the community.

     a.   spirituality
     b.   perspective
     c.   complacency
     d.   decadence
     e.   generosity

3. In her ninth month of pregnancy, Carol ate large quantities of food to _____ her appetite.

   a. dissipate
   b. mitigate
   c. satisfy
   d. solicit
   e. masticate

4. Although she led a(n) _____ life, Sara had a(n) _____ understanding of the world.

   a. urbane - minimal
   b. repetitive - tantalizing
   c. sheltered - unblemished
   d. isolated - simple
   e. prodigious – courageous

5. It was only at age 50, when Steven began to take music lessons, when his _____ talent as an artist began to _____.

   a. considerable - mitigate
   b. meager - wane
   c. latent - emerge
   d. misguided - falter
   e. innate – abrogate

6. Rather than _____ to her mother's wishes, Gayle had the _____ to pursue her own path.

   a. nullify - beneficence
   b. object - audacity
   c. adhere - courage
   d. concede - propensity
   e. panegyrize – execration

7. The _____ woman actually believed that she was Joan of Arc, despite all evidence to the contrary.

   a. innovative
   b. delusional
   c. provocative
   d. vainglorious
   e. temerarious

8. The relationship between the warring spouses was _____ at best.

   a. contentious
   b. dauntless
   c. calumniate
   d. subdued
   e. culpable

9. Although the physician had _____ credentials, the patient was convinced he was a(n) _____.

   a. dubious - maverick
   b. impressive - humanitarian
   c. contradictory - fraud
   d. prestigious - charlatan
   e. mediocre- advocate

10. The designer employed a(n) _____ style, which combined different colors, styles and periods.

    a. eccentric
    b. luxuriant
    c. eclectic
    d. whimsical
    e. flippant

11. Sheila's _____ to alcohol _____ her chances for a promotion at work.

    a. addiction - mediated
    b. predisposition- alleviated
    c. resistance – obscured
    d. aversion – aggrandized
    e. proclivity – sabotaged

12. Ovarian cancer is a(n) _____ disease, because it cannot be diagnosed until an advanced stage, when the chance of survival is _____.

    a. insidious - minimal
    b. pervasive - infinitesimal
    c. virulent - optimistic
    d. tenacious - slim
    e. aggressive – progressive

13. Beth remained _____ for many months after her mother's funeral.

    a. fluvial
    b. inimical
    c. inculcate
    d. promontory
    e. plaintive

14. Greta's _____ wardrobe belies her _____ nature.

    a. paltry - lucid
    b. garish - valorous
    c. sophisticated - simple
    d. practical -multifaceted
    e. juvenile – lowly

15. The mood at the airport became _____ when the news of the crash was announced.

    a. pliant
    b. laconic
    c. plethoric
    d. timorous
    e. dolorous

16. A _____ student is far more likely to be admitted to a top college than one who is _____.

    a. Flamboyant – self-deprecating
    b. fortuitous - stalwart
    c. successful - deliberate
    d. diligent - mediocre
    e. zealous – duplicitous

17. Jeffrey demonstrated great _____ when he left the security of his homeland in search of a better life.

    a. discretion
    b. wanderlust
    c. courage
    d. volatility
    e. repression

18. Bill's rare combination of skills _____ his _____ salary.

    a. sparked - disappointing
    b. minimized - ample
    c. induced - judicious
    d. belied - competitive
    e. justified – astronomical

19. After years of living on her own, Jennifer is 100% _____.

    a. disheartened
    b. captivating
    c. self-reliant
    d. callous
    e. obstinate

20. Diane's _____ at her engagement party was _____ by the realization that she could not marry her boyfriend until after college.

    a. apprehension - inspired
    b. jubilation - enhanced
    c. elation - tempered
    d. distress - erased
    e. turmoil – moderated

Answers to Sentence Completion Questions

1. The correct word means psychic, which is choice C, clairvoyant.

2. The correct word means selflessness, which is choice E, generosity.

3. The missing word means to satisfy, which is choice C.

4. The two words are opposites; the best choices is A, urbane – minimal.

5. The first word means natural or hidden, while the second means appeared. The correct choice is C latent-emerge.

6. The first word means honor or obey, while the second means courage. The correct choice is C, adhere-courage.

7. The correct choice means mentally unbalanced or confused, which is choice B, delusional.

8. The correct answer is a synonym for warring, which is A, contentious.

9. The words will be opposites of each other; the correct choice is D, prestigious- charlatan.

10. The correct word means includes many styles, or choice C, eclectic.

11. The words are opposites; the best answer is choice E, proclivity – sabotaged.

12. The first word is negative, while the second means slim; the correct choice is A, insidious – minimal.

13. The correct answer means sad, which is choice E, plaintive.

14. The two words are opposites; the correct answer is choice C, sophisticated – simple.

15. The correct word is choice E, dolorous, which means extremely sad.

16. The first word means hardworking, while the second word means lazy; the best answer is choice D, diligent – mediocre.

17. The correct word means courage, which is choice C.

18. The two words support each other; the best answer is choice E, justified – astronomical.

19. The word means independent, which is choice C, self-reliant.

20. The first word is positive, while the second is negative; the correct choice is C, elation – tempered.

Chapter 4: Analogies & Antonyms

The Verbal section of the GRE contains 7 **analogy** questions and 9 **antonym** questions, which test the depth and breadth of a student's vocabulary. By studying the word lists in Appendices 2 - 4, you will be well prepared for the most common tricks and traps the test writers use. This chapter will briefly cover a few additional strategies for analogy and antonym questions.

The question stem in an analogy question presents two words in the following manner:

First Word: Second Word::

The single colon (:) between the two terms means "is related to"
The double colon (::) after the pair of words means "in the same way that"

Hence, your job with an analogy question is to:

a) discover the relationship between the first two words
b) find another pair of words that is related in the same way

Example:

SAND: DUNE::

   a.   organs: body
   b.   stars: galaxy
   c.   instrument: orchestra
   d.   eggs : omelet
   e.   granules: sugar

Choice B is correct. A dune is composed of millions of individual grains of sand. Likewise, a galaxy is composed of millions of individual stars.

To answer analogy questions, use the following strategies.

Strategy 1. Before you look at the answer choices, think of a short sentence that describes the relationship between the two words.

Example: RACKET: TENNIS.   *A racket is used to play tennis*

Thus, we must find the pair of words that can be substituted for the original pair.

   a.   type : book
   b.   ball : soccer
   c.   glove : baseball
   d.   club : golf
   e.   board : chess

In this case, our sentence *"A racket is used to play tennis"* only eliminates Choice A. The other choices are still possibilities.

Strategy 2. If more than one answer choice fits your paraphrase, make your statement more specific. In this case, we must more clearly define the relationship between the words racket and tennis: *A racket is used to strike a ball in the game of tennis.* This more specific sentence allows us to eliminate all the answers except Choice D. Just as a club is used to strike a golf ball, a racket is used to strike a tennis ball.

Strategy 3. When you evaluate the answer choices, consider the meaning of each word. In difficult analogy problems, the test writers often use the rare or esoteric meanings of words. How can you tell if a word is being used in an odd way? The parts of speech in an analogy problem will be consistent throughout the problem. If the original pair of words uses a noun and an adjective, then the five answer choices will also use a noun and adjective in the same order.

When you evaluate an answer pair, determine how each word is being used. On the GRE, the following words are often used as both nouns *and* verbs:

curb	document	table	harbor	play	chalk
rent	steep	flower	bolt	fake	brush
champion	air	bustle	blossom	advocate	slip

FIRE: ICE::

    a.   desiccant: silica
    b.   accelerate: table
    c.   marry: join
    d.   aria: harmony
    e.   recoup: salvage

The original words are antonyms; consequently, the correct answer choice will also include words that have opposite meanings. The correct answer is choice B – in this case, the word table means to postpone, which is the opposite of accelerate.

Strategy 4. Carefully scrutinize answer pairs that *remind* you of the original pair, but have a different relationship. The correct answer pair will have the same relationship as the original pair, but the words in the answer will usually be in an entirely different category.

EXCERPT: NOVEL ::

    a.   critique : play
    b.   review : manuscript
    c.   swatch : cloth
    d.   forward : preface
    e.   recital : performance

The correct answer to this problem is C. An excerpt is part of a novel, just as a swatch is part of a cloth. However, many test takers are distracted by choices B and D, which contain words that ALSO relate to novels.

Strategy 5. Be aware of the most common *types of analogies* that appear on the test. Nearly every question on the GRE will include one of the following categories.

Synonyms: the words have similar meanings

               clothing: garments
               industrious: conscientious
               fast: expeditious
               apprehensive: worried
               buoyant: cheerful

Antonyms: the words have opposite meanings

               chivalrous: rude
               honest: deceptive
               intrepid: fearful
               original: derivative
               clarity: confusion

Member and class: one word is a type or example of the other

        Cadillac: automobile
        poodle: dog
        boot: shoe
        apple: fruit
        robbery: crime

Different Intensity: one word is stronger than the other

        walk: run
        drizzle: rain
        like: love
        pretty: beautiful
        trickle: flood

Part to a whole: one word is a type or subset of the other

        professors: faculty
        page: book
        chemistry: science
        employees: staff
        bean: vegetable

Lack of / Absence of: those who are X, do not have Y

        anonymous: name
        destitute: wealth
        healthy: illness
        ignorant: wisdom
        energetic: lethargy

Function or purpose: you use X to accomplish Y

        pencil: write
        automobile: drive
        hyphen: join
        scissors: cut
        stove: cook

Action and significance: X is evidence of Y

        smile: happiness
        frown: disappointment
        handshake: greeting
        money: wealth
        generosity: kindness

Pertaining to: X is the study of Y

        enology: wine
        forensics: crime
        agronomy: soil
        biology: life
        geology: rocks

Symbol and representation: we use X to denote Y

period: stop
brackets: enclose
comma: pause
clapping: enthusiasm
wave: greeting

Different Connotations of words: X is another word for Y

interrogate: question
conspire: collaborate
expire: cease
clever: ingenious
avid: eager

Cause and effect: X causes Y

sun: skin cancer
overeating: obesity
debt: bankruptcy
dedication: success
studying: knowledge

Product and source: X is made from Y

curtains: cloth
window: glass
tire: rubber
veil: lace
shoe: leather

Spatial order: X is the ending of Y

epilogue: story
death: life
conclusion: novel
credits: movie
curtain call: play

Time order: you must X before you can Y

outline: essay
blueprint: house
crawl: walk
sow: reap
earn: spend

Worker and tool: a person in profession X uses Y to do his job

musician: piano
artist: paintbrush
janitor: broom
seamstress: thread
plumber: auger

Worker and workplace: job X is performed in location Y

        lawyer: courtroom
        nurse: hospital
        farmer : field
        teacher: classroom
        astronaut: space ship

Worker and creation: professional X creates product Y

        artist: sketch
        architect: blueprint
        author: novel
        musician: symphony
        seamstress: clothing

Action to object: to accomplish X, you must use Y

        play: piano
        drive: car
        clean: broom
        wash: cloth
        sever: knife

Strategy 6. Boost your **vocabulary**. Analogies are probably the hardest type of question to improve on, because they depend on the inherent strength of your vocabulary. Before the test, review the words in Appendices 2 - 4, which include:

a) the 180 most common words featured on the GRE (definitions plus illustrative sentences)
b) groups of related words
c) tricky look-alike words that test makers love
d) the most common roots, prefixes and suffixes for GRE vocabulary words

If you don't know the precise definition of the word in capital letters, an approximate definition will probably be sufficient. Most words are built or derived from other words with which you may be more familiar:

a) tempestuous   Related Words temper
b) perturbation   Related Word: perturbed
c) severance   Related Word: sever

Strategy 7. If you cannot identify the root of an unknown word, try to put the word in some sort of context. When we speak, we use words in phrases in sentences, rather than in isolation. Yet words that we understand fully in sentences may appear unfamiliar when we view them out of context. When you see a word on the GRE, put it in a familiar context to better understand its meaning.

a) savant   "idiot savant"   means genius
b) gratuitous   "gratuitous violence"   means unnecessary
c) requiem   "requiem for a heavyweight"   means a rest

Strategy 8. Test the unknown word for positive or negative connotations.

a) Any word that starts with "de-", "dis-" or "anti-" is usually negative. This includes degradation, discrepancy, debase, antipathy

b) Words that include the concept of going up are usually positive, while those that include the concept of going down are usually negative.

Positive examples: elevate, ascend, adulation, illustrious

Strategy 9. Watch out for words that look similar, but have different meanings. Appendix 3 has dozens of examples of tricky look-alike words that the test writers love, including:

ambulance/ambulatory	suffer/suffrage	friend/fiend
platitude/gratitude	inspired/insipid	vicious/viscous
noble/ignoble	ingenious/ingenuous	waiver/waver

Strategy 10. Now that you've learned the strategies, try the following questions. The answers are presented at the end of the chapter.

1. **HYPHEN: JOIN::**

    a. Knife: cut
    b. Sentence: explain
    c. Ocean: boat
    d. Newspaper: edit
    e. Mirror: frame

2. **HYPOCRITICAL: DISINGENUOUS::**

    a. Enigmatic: concise
    b. Ingenious: clever
    c. Distant: excessive
    d. Equitable: endogamous
    e. Banal: original

3. **DEBT: BANKRUPTCY::**

    a. Alcohol: inebriation
    b. Rain: meteorology
    c. Ice cream: dairy
    d. Clothing: underwear
    e. Money: spending

4. **PREVARICATE: EVADE::**

    a. Cryptic: cogent
    b. Sardonic: compassionate
    c. Irascible: mellow
    d. Fortuitous: noisome
    e. Inchoate: amorphous

5. **EARN: SPEND::**

    a. Advocate: litigate
    b. Crawl: walk
    c. Borrow: buy
    d. Spell: speak
    e. Laugh: cry

6. **AUTHOR: MANSCRIPT::**

    a. Actor: role
    b. Administrator: office
    c. Soldier: weapon
    d. Software engineer: code
    e. Astronaut: rocket

7. **FINE: EXTRAORDINARY::**

    a. Malinger: illness
    b. Simile: metaphor
    c. Gregarious: misanthrope
    d. Impervious: rare
    e. Losing: defeat

8. **CONTAMINATED: PURE::**

    a. Unlikely: know
    b. Soluble: float
    c. Incredible: prove
    d. Stationary: moving
    e. Articulate: amoral

9. **TAXATION: WEALTH::**

    a. Truth: corruption
    b. Dieting: weight
    c. Insanity: medication
    d. Misrepresentation: lawsuit
    e. Speed: duration

10. **SKEIN: YARN::**

    a. Package: peanuts
    b. Hub cap : wheel
    c. Ball: string
    d. Revolution: tire
    e. Thread: spool

11. **ANODYNE: INSIPID::**

    a. Charismatic: wan
    b. Derivative: innovative
    c. Centrifuge: separation
    d. Exhilarating: heady
    e. Nuclei: electron

12. **MEDDLE: DISREGARD::**

    a. Sully: purify
    b. Membrane: divide
    c. Spontaneous: unexpected
    d. Cantankerous: tetchy
    e. Void: abyss

13. **SANTA: SLEIGH::**

    a. Ghost: nightmare
    b. Admiral: ship
    c. Bunny: Easter
    d. Pilot: airport
    e. Songs: carols

14. **CARBUNCLE: BOIL::**

    a. Mark: commemorate
    b. Injury: diagnose
    c. Demur: dainty
    d. Consequence: fatal
    e. Memory: enhance

15. **CLOWN: SERIOUS::**

    a. Runner: sprint
    b. Psychologist: analyze
    c. Reporter: uninformed
    d. Policeman: lawful
    e. Attorney: advocate

16. **FORENSICS: CRIME::**

    a. Instrumentation: analyses
    b. Geology: seismology
    c. Cosmetology: beauty
    d. Weather: meteorology
    e. Geography: seasons

17. **MUTED: SUBDUED::**

    a. Ginger: auburn
    b. Mountain: molehill
    c. Character: personable
    d. Immoral: destitute
    e. Spiritual: nascent

18. **INACTIVITY: ATROPHY::**

    a. Growth: death
    b. Melting: warmth
    c. Exercise: melancholy
    d. Debt: insolvency
    e. Dedication: insight

19. **DEXTERITY: SCULPTOR::**

    a. Persuasiveness: salesman
    b. Justice: prosecutor
    c. Fertilizer: farmer
    d. Animals: veterinarian
    e. Cowardice: fearful

20. **QUIBBLE: DISSEMBLE::**

   a. Amalgamate: negotiate
   b. Correspondence: documentation
   c. Proactive: remedial
   d. Fortitude: infirmity
   e. Tractable: polite

Answer Key for Analogy Questions

1 You must use X to accomplish Y. Choice A is correct.

2. The words are synonyms. Choice B is correct.

3. The first word causes the second. Choice A is correct.

4. The words are synonyms. Choice E is correct.

5. You must do X before you can Y. Choice B is correct.

6. X creates Y. Choice D is correct.

7. The first word is a less intense version of the second word. Choice E is correct.

8. Something that is X cannot be Y. Choice D is correct.

9. The first word reduces the second. Choice B is correct.

10. X is a long, unbroken, rolled-up quantity of Y. Choice C is correct.

11. The words are synonyms. Choice D is correct.

12. The words are antonyms. Choice A is correct.

13. X travels via Y. Choice B is correct.

14. The words are synonyms. Choice A is correct.

15. X does not show Y emotion/activity. Choice C is correct.

16. X is the study of Y. Choice C is correct.

17. The words are synonyms. Choice A is correct.

18. The second word is a consequence of the first word. Choice D is correct.

19. The first word is a skill that is used by the second word. Choice A is correct.

20. The words are synonyms. Choice E is correct.

Antonyms

The GRE will also contain 9 Antonym questions, in which you will be asked to select the word that means the *opposite* of a given word. For these questions, you should use all of the strategies that we have already mentioned for analogy questions, along with the following:

Strategy 10. Define the word - and predict the meaning of its opposite. Whenever possible, you should have an idea of what you're looking for before you check the answer choices. From our experience, this has a tangible benefit on your score. By consciously predicting an answer, you will lessen the chance of selecting a synonym of the stem word, rather than an antonym (which is one of the most common mistakes on the exam).

ABRIDGE:

    a.   dissent
    b.   assail
    c.   unfetter
    d.   consolidate
    e.   protrude

Abridge means to shorten. The opposite is distend, which means to swell or protrude. Choice E is correct. As you probably expect, the incorrect answer choices included possible traps. Choice D is a synonym of abridge, rather than an antonym – it is there to confuse you. Likewise, Choice A (dissent) is also a trap because it sounds like the word distend, which is what we are looking for. Be careful.

Strategy 11. Find the answer choice that best matches your prediction. Check all the choices for the best fit. If necessary, consider alternative definitions for the stem word.

FACE:

    a.   epidermis
    b.   podiatry
    c.   circumvent
    d.   ventral
    e.   countenance

In this example, the word face means to acknowledge or handle. The opposite is circumvent, Choice C, which is to ignore something or someone.

From our experience, this is the type of question that tricks students who fail to consider the alternative use of the stem word. By including alternative answer choices that relate to the physical meaning of the word face, the test writers subtly reinforce the wrong answer.

Strategy 12. Use intelligent elimination strategies. First, eliminate answer choices that have no clear "opposite." Next, eliminate any words that are synonyms of the given word. If two (or more) choices have the same meaning, eliminate both - there is only one correct answer for antonyms questions (and it will not be ambiguous).

TENACITY:

    a.   simplicity
    b.   chicanery
    c.   persistence
    d.   sentience
    e.   flexibility

Choice E is correct. Tenacity means stubborn or persistent. Flexibility is its opposite.

Strategy 13. Use the "sense" of a word to eliminate probable wrong answers: if the stem is positive, the correct answer will be negative, and vice versa.

CYNICISM:

    a.   delusion
    b.   fascism
    c.   remorse
    d.   sarcasm
    e.   sanguine

In this case, Choice E is correct. Cynicism means pessimistic or sarcastic. The opposite is buoyant or sanguine. But, if you didn't know the meaning of the words, you could probably have narrowed down your choices simply by how they sound. The word cynicism sounds negative, as do answer choices A, B, C, and D. Sanguine, on the other hand, sounds neutral, or at least *different* from the other choices. The "sound it out" technique isn't foolproof, but it is worth considering for questions in which you have little - if anything - to go on.

Strategy 14. At the risk of sounding like a broken record, *review the groups of words in Appendix 2 (and their opposites).* Many of the words on the antonym section of the GRE appear on these lists. Appendix 2b, in particular, is well worth your perusal – it gives 50 popular antonym pairs of words that are favorites of the test writers. If you took the GRE today, how many would you get right?

Strategy 15. Now that you've learned the strategies, try your hand at the following sample questions. The answers are provided at the end of the chapter.

1. **DECAMP:**

    a.   Glamorize
    b.   Crave
    c.   Approach
    d.   Abandon
    e.   Vilify

2. **PERIPATETIC:**

    a.   Clear
    b.   Wise
    c.   Soiled
    d.   Laconic
    e.   Stationary

3. **HECTOR:**

    a.   Solitary
    b.   Innocent
    c.   Tyro
    d.   Encourage
    e.   Fulsome

4. **ABERRATION**:

    a. Eccentric
    b. Normal
    c. Diurnal
    d. Wicked
    e. Superior

5. **STULTIFY**:

    a. Assuage
    b. Vilify
    c. Vindicate
    d. Accentuate
    e. Meander

6. **PROLIX**:

    a. Concise
    b. Dim
    c. Unassuming
    d. Barren
    e. Forthright

7. **ANCILLARY**:

    a. Additional
    b. Prerequisite
    c. Outside
    d. Primary
    e. Miraculous

8. **ASPERITY**:

    a. Wealth
    b. Destitution
    c. Austerity
    d. Bland
    e. Softness

9. **NOMINAL**:

    a. Original
    b. Derivative
    c. Actual
    d. Anonymous
    e. Unexpected

10. **OBLIQUE**:

    a. Muscular
    b. Circuitous
    c. Opaque
    d. Concave
    e. Upright

11. **PLIABLE:**

    a. Rigid
    b. Supple
    c. Essential
    d. Original
    e. Respectable

12. **DISPASSIONATE**:

    a. Detached
    b. Fiery
    c. Unbiased
    d. Insensitive
    e. Obtuse

13. **VACILLATE**:

    a. Restrain
    b. Waiver
    c. Abscond
    d. Waver
    e. Decide

14. **SAGE**:

    a. Mystic
    b. Simpleton
    c. Scholar
    d. Bland
    e. Confused

15. **UNERRING**:

    a. Definitive
    b. Fashionable
    c. Faulty
    d. Repetitive
    e. Polished

16. **ACME**:

    a. Nadir
    b. Zenith
    c. Chaotic
    d. Paramount
    e. Placid

17. **CONCLAVE:**

    a. Assembly
    b. Solitary
    c. Convex
    d. Caucus
    e. Infirmity

18. **ABASE**:

    a. Snivel
    b. Humiliate
    c. Extol
    d. Circumvent
    e. Annoy

19. **ANTITHESIS**:

    a. Parallel
    b. Opposite
    c. Conclusion
    d. Partner
    e. Codicil

20. **CENSURE**:

    a. Reduce
    b. Praise
    c. Litigate
    d. Repudiate
    e. Discourteous

Answer Key for Antonym Questions

1. Decamp means to escape or flee, which is the opposite of approach. Choice C is correct.

2. Peripatetic means roaming or nomadic, which is the opposite of stationary. Choice E is correct.

3. Hector means to bully or harass, which is the opposite of encourage. Choice D is correct.

4. Aberration means deviation or anomaly, which is the opposite of normal. Choice B is correct.

5. Stultify means to reduce or dampen, which is the opposite of accentuate. Choice D is correct.

6. Prolix means wordy or verbose, which is the opposite of concise. Choice A is correct.

7. Ancillary means auxiliary or supplementary, which is the opposite of primary. Choice D is correct.

8. Asperity means roughness or severity, which is the opposite of softness. Choice E is correct.

9. Nominal means supposed or ostensible, which is the opposite of actual. Choice C is correct.

10. Oblique means slanted or tilted, which is the opposite of upright. Choice E is correct.

11. Pliable means elastic or supple, which is the opposite of rigid. Choice A is correct.

12. Dispassionate means calm or cool, which is the opposite of fiery. Choice B is correct.

13. Vacillate means to waver or hesitate, which is the opposite of decide. Choice E is correct.

14. Sage means scholarly or intellectual, which is the opposite of a simpleton. Choice B is correct.

15. Unerring means correct or certain, which is the opposite of faulty. Choice C is correct.

16. Acme means peak or top, which is the opposite of nadir. Choice A is correct.

17. A conclave is a meeting or assembly, which is the opposite of solitary. Choice B is correct.

18. Abase means to degrade or belittle, which is the opposite of praise or extol. Choice C is correct.

19. Antithesis means opposite or reverse, which is the opposite of parallel. Choice A is correct.

20. Censure means fault or criticize, which is the opposite of praise. Choice B is correct.

Chapter 5. Reading Comprehension

The Verbal section of the GRE includes two or three short passages, followed by 8 Reading Comprehension questions. Although the passages could theoretically be about any subject, the most common themes are politics, history, science, business and the humanities. By design, the test writers try to choose material that does not favor any particular college major.

Most readers find the passages difficult because the subject matter is dry and obscure. Indeed, many of them are excerpts from academic journals, which favor a formal writing style, the passive verb tense and esoteric, hard-to-pronounce words. Passages are never re-printed verbatim, though. Instead, the original article is heavily edited to just one-quarter to one-third of its original length, to retain the formal style of the piece.

Unfortunately, this severe editing also makes the passages quite dense, because it removes most of the elements that enhance readability, such as the introduction, descriptive fillers and transitional phrases. Even worse, the passages often start in the middle of an explanation or discussion, which forces the reader to jump in with no clear point of reference.

Why did the test writers choose such difficult material? To determine if you can quickly identify the objective and logic of a cumbersome piece of writing and apply the author's premise to new situations. Clearly, to answer the questions correctly in the rigid timeframe, you must read the passages with a different mindset than you use in most traditional coursework.

Here are the directions for the Reading Comprehension section of the GRE:

Directions: Each passage in this group is followed by questions based on its content. After reading its content, choose the best answer to each question, based on what is stated or implied in the passage and any introductory material that may be provided.

Strategy 1. Unlike other sections of the GRE, the questions (and passages) in the Reading Comprehension section are NOT arranged in the order of difficulty. Since all questions are worth the same, you should start with the passage that seems easiest to YOU. Choose the passage that is about a subject of interest to you.... or that seems particularly easy to understand. Set yourself up to succeed.

Once you pick your first passage, take your time and answer ALL of the questions for it. Remember, this is your "easiest" one; get as many questions right before you move onto the next passage. If no particular passage seems "easier" than the others, start with the one that has the most questions. By doing so, you can tackle more questions upfront, when you are fresh and alert.

Strategy 2. Before reading the entire passage, we recommend that you give it a *quick (90 seconds or less) overview.* Read the italicized information first. It will put the passage into a perspective or context that is essential for you to understand.

Then:

a. Circle the important nouns in the passage. From our perspective, an "important" noun is a formal name, a place, or other frequently used word that indicates the overall topic of the passage and the different ideas or themes that are being discussed. By quickly circling the important nouns, you will be familiar with them (and where they occur) when you subsequently read the passage.
b. *Draw a box* around any *transitional words* that indicate that the author is changing directions. These are critical for questions about details in the passage;

Words that amplify an idea: *And, also, in addition, additionally, too, or, besides, moreover, furthermore, therefore, in fact, the use of a colon or semi-colon.*

Words that dispute an idea: *But, ironically, nevertheless, however, instead, yet, despite, in spite of, nonetheless, unless, although, not, except, while, rather, on the other hand.*

Words that suggest cause and effect: *Because, therefore, as a result, consequently, since, so, by, accordingly, when.*

These transitional words show where the author amplifies a point, changes direction, or indicates cause and effect. Consequently, they are natural places for questions to be drawn. The test writers form questions at these junctures to test whether or not you followed the author's line of reasoning or got lost along the way. For this reason, they also include an incorrect answer choice that is the exact OPPOSITE of the correct answer. From our experience, sentences that contain transitional words nearly ALWAYS contain the answer to a test question.

c. Underline the main idea, which will be located in one of three places:

The first line of paragraph one
The last line of paragraph one
The last line of the entire passage

Don't waste a lot of time on the overview; the entire process, which includes reading the italicized information, circling the important nouns and finding the main idea, should take **90 seconds or less.**

Strategy 3. In test prep classes, many students ask us whether they should read the questions before they read the actual passage, so that they will be better prepared to find the answers. **Absolutely not.** Once again, the beauty of the GRE is its predictability. Although the passages may be on a variety of topics, the questions will inevitably fall into one of four categories:

Main Idea
Specific Details and Word Meanings (line reference questions)
Reasoning and Implications
Tone or Mood of the Passage

Ironically, the key to performing well on this section is not your particular reading technique, but your familiarity with these four types of questions.

Strategy 4. After you complete your 90-second overview, read the passage in its entirety. Then, nail the main idea question, which tests your ability to identify and understand the author's intent. Main idea questions are usually the first ones in each question set. Some common main idea questions are:

Which of the following best expresses the main idea of the passage?
The primary purpose of the passage is to ...
In the passage, the author's primary concern is to discuss. ..
Which of the following would be an excellent title for the passage?

Because main idea questions are relatively easy, the test writers try to obscure the correct answer by surrounding it with close answer choices that either overstate or understate the author's view. Answers that stress specifics tend to *understate* the main idea or only relate to a particular paragraph in the passage. Likewise, other choices will add new information or go beyond the scope of the passage; by doing so, they *overstate* the main idea. Other tempting incorrect answer choices are "half-right and half-wrong;" they incorporate some of the author's ideas, but are not a complete match. The correct answer will:

a. Re-state the author's idea in a new way, without adding additional details
b. Be similar in scope to the original passage
c. Relate to the *entire* passage, not just an individual paragraph
d. Be a rational, measured response, rather than an extreme view

Ninety percent of the time, the main idea of a passage is found in the first paragraph or in the final sentence of the entire passage.

Strategy 5. After you answer the main idea question, proceed to the questions that include **specific line references**. When answering this type of question, don't rely on memory. Go back and re-read that actual line from which the question is drawn. The correct answer must refer directly to the statement in the passage, not to something implied by it.

The writers have two predictable traps for line reference questions. First, they include incorrect answer choices that refer directly to the passage (almost verbatim), but do not answer the question. These choices can be tempting, because they repeat words and phrases that seem familiar to the student. Second, the questions are often chosen from points in the passage where a key transition has just occurred. If the student does not notice the transitional word (such as *but, however*, or *yet*), (s)he will fall into a wrong answer trap.

A general rule of thumb; the correct answer is rarely located on the line that is mentioned in the question stem. Most of the time, it is located a few lines before or after the line that is mentioned.

<u>Example</u>: if the question asks about something on Line 21, the answer can be found anywhere from Line 18 to Line 24. Focus your attention there; it is extremely rare for an answer to be anywhere else.

Strategy 6. Ironically, although the GRE writers do not present the Reading Comprehension questions in the order of difficulty, they ARE presented in the order in which the answers are located in the passage. For example, if question 2 asks about a reference in Line 16, then question 3 will relate to information that is found AFTER Line 16 in the passage. Likewise, if the answer to question 3 is on Line 24, the answer to question 4 will be found AFTER Line 24 in the passage. Unfortunately, the detailed nature of the test questions WILL force you to go back and re-read certain parts of the passage. Don't waste time searching for something in the wrong place.

Here are typical question stems for line reference questions:

In line 16, the author mentions his experience in the woods in order to……
In line 26, the three films are actually references to…..
In line 34, the word "mirage" most nearly means…

Strategy 7. Many questions will ask you to explain the meaning of a word that the author has used in a specific line of the passage. In many cases, the word in question will have multiple meanings; your task is to identify its meaning in the context of this particular passage. As you might expect, the incorrect answer choices will likely include other meanings of the same word.

<u>Example</u>: if the word in question is "modest," it could mean either small or shy. Expect to see several synonyms of the WRONG meaning in the answer choices.

Watch for unusual or uncommon usage of words. Students sometimes overlook points in a passage because a familiar word is used in an unfamiliar manner. An example is *champion*. As a noun, champion means a hero or accomplished person. Yet, the word can also be used as a verb, in which it is a synonym for *support* or *advocate*.

Once you choose an answer to a question about a word's meaning, go back to the original passage and substitute in the answer you have chosen. Confirm that it makes sense. This simple step will only take you a minute (or less), but will ensure that you haven't made a contextual error.

Strategy 8. If a question asks what something **"infers," "implies," or "suggests,"** it is asking you to dig deeper into the meaning of the author's opinion or thoughts. Reasoning and implication questions require you to go **beyond** what is stated in the passage to draw an inference, make a conclusion, or identify the author's unstated assumptions.

It can be inferred from the passage that. ..
The passage suggests that. ..
From this we can conclude that.....

Since reasoning and implication questions require you to go beyond the passage, the correct answer must say **more** than what is stated in the passage. Although it will not require a quantum leap in thought, the correct answer will add significantly to the ideas presented in the passage.

Sometimes, the writers will ask you to apply what you have learned from the passage to a different or hypothetical situation.

What is the most likely source of the passage?
The author would most likely agree with which one of the following statements?
Which one of the following sentences would best complete the last paragraph of the passage?

To answer this type of question, you should NOT consider your own opinions or personal experiences on the topic. Consider only the **author's** perspective in the passage. Ask yourself:

what is he arguing for?
what might make his argument stronger?
what might make it weaker?

The correct answer choice will build on the author's view without wandering off-track or introducing inconsistent or unexpected ideas.

Strategy 9. In many cases, the test writers will ask you to identify the **tone** of a passage, which is the author's mood, attitude and perspective. Does (s)he feel positive, negative or neutral? Does (s)he give his/her own opinion or present those of others? Is (s)he calm or emotional?

Before reading the answer choices, decide whether the writer's tone is positive, negative or neutral. If you didn't get a feel for the writer's attitude on your first reading, check the adjectives that (s)he uses (they nearly always have a positive or negative connotation).

One helpful tip is to eliminate any extreme answer choices. As a general rule, the GRE uses academic passages that are not overly emotional. So, answer choices such as "jubilant," "exhilarating" and "invigorating" will rarely be correct. Likewise, the test writers rarely use passages that are overly negative or pessimistic in tone, which means that answer choices such as "despondent," "defiant," "suicidal," "hostile," and "catastrophic" will rarely be correct.

Invariably, the correct answer choice will be a neutral word, or one that indicates a reasonable level of emotion (such as "respectful," "indifferent," "tolerant," "unbiased," "ambivalent," "encouraged").

The ONLY exceptions to this rule are excerpts from novels that contain significant dialogue in which the characters don't simply speak, but "cry" or "exclaim." Although these emotional passages are extremely rare on the GRE, they occur often enough to warrant mentioning.

When you choose your correct answer to a tone question, go back to the original passage and find other words to validate your choice. With rare exceptions, the tone of the passage will parallel the main idea. If the author's intent is to explain the reasons for abolishing slavery, the tone will be explanatory or encouraging, not negative or discouraging. Finally, the correct answer to a tone question will never be vague, controversial or grammatically questionable. When you review the passage for supporting terms, it will feel instinctively "right."

Strategy 10. When the answer choices for a tone question includes five PAIRS of words, immediately eliminate any combinations that make no sense, such as "cautiously hostile," "condescendingly apathetic," or "predictably unique." The correct answer choice will be **never** be something odd, vague or confusing.

Invariably, the correct answer will be the combination of words in which the first word appropriately qualifies the second. Further, the combination will be a logical phrase that captures the overall attitude of the writer. Examples of logical pairs of adjectives:

cautiously optimistic   insightful observation
qualified admiration   calculated self-interest
natural affinity

Strategy 11. A final type of question in the Reading Comprehension section is the "reverse" format, in which the question stem includes either NOT or EXCEPT in all capital letters. The questions will ask you to select the piece of information that was NOT given or the idea that the author would NOT agree with. These "reverse" type questions tend to be harder than other types, because of the odd way that the questions are phrased.

Remember, if the question asks which piece of information was NOT mentioned in the passage, the four incorrect answer choices will all sound familiar, because you have already seen similar words and ideas in the passage. This is one time when the answer with new or different information WILL be correct.

Here's another helpful tip for "reverse" questions:": one of the writers' most common tricks is to put the *exact opposite* of the correct answer as one of the answer choices. They are trying to set a trap for test takers who get confused by the word EXCEPT, and pick the opposite response.

So, as you review the answer choices for this type of question, pay particular attention to answer choices that are exact opposites of each other. One of them is the right answer and the other is the trap. The good news is that you can usually narrow your selection to these two choices. Then, calmly evaluate what you are being asked and choose accordingly.

Strategy 12. For **all** question types, be wary of extreme answers that contain "all or nothing" words such as *must, always, impossible, never, cannot, each, every, totally, all, solely and only*. Few passages will be written in such an absolute tone, which means that these extreme answer choices will rarely be correct.

Strategy 13. If you get pressed for time, finish all of the questions for a single passage before you move onto the next one. If you DO manage to finish ahead of time and come back to a particularly difficult passage, you will probably not be able to "jump back in" without re-reading it. This is why we recommend that you complete the passages in the order in which they interest you. Get as many points on the easy material before you tread into more difficult waters.

Strategy 14. Probably the biggest complaint we hear about the Reading Comprehension section is that students run out of time; often, they get bogged down on a difficult question and wind up with two or three minutes to handle an *entire* passage. Ideally, you will pace yourself on the exam and not find yourself in this sort of jam. If you do, relax and employ this **final emergency strategy**.

More than any other section of the GRE, the Reading Comprehension section offers the chance for a last-ditch end run. How? Let's assume that you only have three minutes to handle the last passage in the section. In that time, you should be able to:

1. Find the main idea question and answer it. Remember, the main idea will be the first or last sentence in the first paragraph or the final sentence in the entire passage. You can probably nail it within 45 seconds.

2. Then, move on to the tone question. Immediately rule out extreme answer choices. Quickly scan the passage for key words to indicate the author's mood or attitude. You've got a great chance of nailing this answer, too.

3. Finally, choose the line reference question that asks you to define a specific word in the passage. Remember, you can determine the answer from context; at worst, you will have to read the two lines before and after the line mentioned in the question stem. You can usually guess the meaning.

4. If you have any time left, try to tackle another line reference question. Do NOT, under any circumstances, try to handle any reasoning or implication questions, which will require you to understand and apply the details of the passage to new situations. Focus instead on picking up a few quick points on the easier questions.

Is this strategy foolproof? No. Sometimes students are so stressed out that they lose their cool (or their concentration). Try to keep your wits. By employing these suggestions, you will have an excellent chance at picking up at least 3 points in less than three minutes. You can also try to eliminate answer choices when you guess at the other questions as well. If you are the type of person who thrives in a crisis, this is the strategy for you!

Strategy 15. Finally, practice as much as you can with sample passages and test questions. The more comfortable you become with the question stems (along with the games the test writers play with answer choices), the more confident you will be on the day of the test. Here are several sample passages. The answers are presented at the end of the chapter.

Passage 1

In theory, governments provide a significant source of a people's collective political identity as well as the main arena in which individuals can organize for political action. Yet, in actuality, the type of government is a key indicator of how effective that political action will be. In the United States, individuals who are frustrated by the presidential system often suggest that Americans would be better served if the U.S. adopted a parliamentary system of government. Although both systems are democratic, the differences between them would create major changes in American politics if the U.S. completely switched over to a parliamentary system. Assuming, for example, that the U.S. adopted a unicameral parliamentary political system with a Proportional Representation (PR) electoral system, its citizens would immediately enjoy greater government efficiency, accountability, an increase in voter turnout and less waste of taxpayer money.

10   The fusion of powers in a parliamentary system creates a supreme legislative, executive, and judicial authority that can develop policies in a straightforward manner, without the checks and balances of a presidential system. In the U.S., where power is fragmented by the separation of powers, Congress is not obligated to pass legislation that the President proposes. Likewise, every bill passed by Congress must be reviewed by the President, who can either veto it or sign it into law. This process, which can be further complicated by the judicial branch, creates significant barriers that can slow down or halt the passage of law.

16   In contrast, the parliamentary system in Great Britain has fused its executive and legislative branches into the cabinet, the controlling and directing body of parliament, which operates by majority rule. To implement policy, the majority party expresses its power through the cabinet to bring about its desired legislation. In effect, if the cabinet enjoys party solidarity, it does not need to wonder if its policy will be stalled in the legislature or other branches of government. As long as the majority of cabinet members support the proposed legislation, parliament can implement policy quickly and effectively.

22   Candidates in a parliamentary system are also more likely to be held accountable for the promises they make when they run for office than candidates in a presidential system. After all, once the majority seizes power in the parliament, they enjoy the complete control of the cabinet. Voters, consequently, know exactly who to blame for their current situation: the party or parties in power. In contrast, voters in a presidential system are seldom sure who to blame because the fragmented system creates so many independent sources of power that an unhappy policy cannot be blamed on any one of them.. As a result, voters who cannot accurately reward or blame their elected officials may vote less on policy-related criteria and more on a candidate's personality.

30   In many countries, the cabinet must report regularly to parliament about how it is managing the affairs of the state, which provides an extra level of accountability that is missing in a presidential system. In Great Britain, the Prime Minister must appear before parliament each week to answer blunt and direct interrogations from the opposition. The U.S. presidential system, however, does not have an equivalent forum in which the executive branch must account for its actions on a regular basis. Sadly, history suggests that when public officials cannot be held accountable, it becomes easier for them to spend public money or initiate policy contrary to their election promises.

37   Changing the U.S. electorate system from a Single Member District Plurality system (SMDP) to a Proportional Representation (PR) would most likely increase voter turnout, because it would eliminate the idea that any individual vote is wasted. In a PR system, people vote for parties, whose percentage of seats in the legislature is equivalent to the percentage of the electoral vote the party receives. To illustrate, picture the United State as one large state consisting of only one

district and only 100 available seats in parliament. Each party running for a seat would create a list of their top 100 members, who would be their potential candidates. However, the number of actual candidates that the party would eventually send to parliament would depend on the percentage of votes that the party received. In this scenario, if a party received 20 percent of the votes in the election, it would secure 20 seats in parliament, which would go to the top 20 candidates on its list. Likewise, if a party received 50 percent of the votes, it would secure 50 seats in parliament, which would go to the top 50 candidates on its list.

48 In contrast, a SMDP system divides the state or country into several districts that have separate elections for their representatives. The resulting legislature includes the candidates who won a plurality of the vote in their respective districts. If the population of a district heavily favors a candidate from one particular party, the people from an opposing or minority party may feel that their vote is wasted, since their candidate can't possibly win the election. Far too often, people get discouraged by the SMDP system and eventually stop voting, which reduces the overall turnout. In a PR system, however, people are more willing to participate because they know that their vote will contribute to a percentage of seats obtained in the legislature, even if their party does not receive the majority of the votes.

56 By eliminating specific district representatives, the PR system would also reduce taxpayer spending on projects that only benefit one district. In the SMDP system, representatives may try to divert state money to pet projects that reward their own districts for their vote. Instead, the PR system features candidate lists that are organized state-wide, whereby candidates envision the nation as a single district whose efficient and effective representation is in their party's best interest. Consequently, the PR system creates a political environment that encourages a spirit of mutuality, rather than selfishness.

62 Although the current system of presidential government in the United States is effective, it could benefit from several of the components in the parliamentary and PR systems. In theory, the parliamentary system offers improved accountability and efficiency, and limits the waste of taxpayer money on pet projects. However, the current U.S. election process is a cherished and deeply entrenched part of American culture that dates back to the Constitution. Despite its inherent flaws, most U.S. citizens are satisfied with the presidential system and are not sufficiently motivated to change. In the absence of a political crisis, it is highly unlikely that Americans will champion the parliamentary system as a viable alternative.

69

1. What is the main point of the passage?

   a. The PR electorate system of government is superior to the presidential system.
   b. With minor concessions, the U.S. can improve its electorate process by adopting certain points of the PR electorate system,
   c. An SMDP electorate system is superior to the PR system.
   d. Although the parliamentary system of government offers several benefits to citizens, the U.S. is unlikely to adopt it in the near future.
   e. The U.S. electorate process offers its citizens a unique set of checks and balances that should not be compromised.

2. In line 2, what does *arena* mean?

   a. chambers
   b. stage
   c. meeting place
   d. stadium
   e. forum

3. According to the passage, U.S. citizens would enjoy many benefits if they adopted a PR electoral system of government. Which of the following is NOT one of those benefits?

    a.   Less waste of taxpayer money
    b.   Greater accountability
    c.   Greater representation for women and minorities
    d.   Increased voter turnout
    e.   Greater government efficiency

4. According to the author, to what can the slow pace of the legislative process in the U.S. be attributed?

    a.   The solidarity of the Cabinet
    b.   the fusion of powers created by a supreme legislative, executive and judicial authority
    c.   the President's right to veto any bill passed by Congress
    d.   the staggered election years for Senators and Congressman, which can affect the support for any given bill
    e.   the tendency of Congressmen to vote along party lines, which creates an adversarial political environment

5. In Great Britain, how are policies passed?

    a.   By special approval of the Prime Minister
    b.   Exclusively by the legislative branch
    c.   by majority rule in all three branches of government
    d.   by majority rule in the cabinet
    e.   by a public election

6. According to the author, why do voters in the U.S. vote according to a candidate's personality?

    a.   they support the special interests of that candidate
    b.   they are more intuitive than citizens in other countries
    c.   they are influenced by political advertisements, which emphasize the candidate's personality traits
    d.   they do not feel that they can hold the candidates accountable for policy success or failure
    e.   they trust their candidates more than citizens in other countries

7. According to the passage, why are British officials less likely to spend public money?

    a.   They are given limited spending authority compared to U.S. officials
    b.   The Prime Minister makes all budgetary decisions
    c.   They are more frugal by nature
    d.   They are given a specific budget each year which cannot be adjusted for any reason
    e.   They must account for their actions on a regular basis

8. Which of the following statements is NOT true about the PR system?

    a.   Each district has a separate election for its representatives
    b.   It eliminates the idea that a single vote is wasted
    c.   People vote for parties, rather than candidates
    d.   It usually increases voter turnout
    e.   The percentage of seats a party receives in the legislature is equivalent to the percentage of the electoral vote the party receives

9. In line 57, what does *pet* mean?

    a. bi-partisan
    b. pork barrel spending
    c. special interest
    d. corrupt
    e. covert

10. According to the author, under what circumstances would the U.S, change its current system of government?

    a. The emergence of a viable third political party
    b. An amendment to the Constitution
    c. A political crisis
    d. To eliminate the national debt
    e. The successful impeachment of the President

Passage 2.

In and of itself, competition can be a healthy ingredient in the workplace, which produces better quality products or services at the lowest possible price. It can also stimulate the search for new technologies or better ways to satisfy customers. Pushed to extremes, however, competition can often reach an intensity that results in unethical practices and detrimental consequences.

5

Such intense competition, along with the desire to maximize profits and personal wealth, lead the formerly successful Enron Corporation down an unethical and illegal path. In the early days, Enron experienced significant growth and gained substantial credibility as a natural gas company. Later on, however, most of its successful operations were replaced by the illusion of successful initiatives. Over time, executives were no longer able to generate large profits, and, in fact, gambled away a substantial part of the company's financial resources. As a result, Enron's top executives began to actively borrow funds from Wall Street investors to make up the difference. The company's financial deficits, however, were effectively hidden from the investment bankers, as well as the remainder of the financial community.

14

As a result of many unwise and unethical domestic and foreign investments, extravagant corporate expenditures by the enterprise's top executives and a series of scandals involving irregular mark-to-market accounting procedures, Enron filed the largest bankruptcy in the American history on December 2, 2001.

18

Most people don't realize that Enron, like many other American corporations, possessed its very own Code of Ethics, in which the company tried to position itself as an international employer, a creator of innovative energy solutions, as well as a global corporate citizen. It assured all of its employees that these great responsibilities were not taken lightly by the corporation's executive management, which was committed to conducting itself in a respectful manner. The Code of Ethics continued to explain that Enron felt very strongly about its core values; it demanded that its employees treat each other as they would like to be treated themselves. Further, the Code of Ethics emphasized the importance of honoring all promises to clients and corporate prospects. Finally, it listed open communication and excellence at the top of its list of core values. Most impressively, all employees, including executive managers, were held to the same standards in respect to the company's vision and values. As required by most firms, Enron also mandated a signed compliance form that verified that each employee would adhere to the stipulated corporate standards.

30

Upon the approval of the company's Board of Directors, Enron's Chairman, Kenneth Lay presented the Code of Ethics in July 2000. Ironically, on May 25th, 2006, Mr. Lay was convicted of one count of conspiracy, three counts of securities fraud, three counts of bank fraud and two wire fraud counts. In addition, Mr. Lay was found guilty of signing misleading audit representation letters and making false statements and presentations to securities analysts and rating agencies.

36

Subsequently, Jeffrey K. Skilling, Enron's former Chief Executive Officer since February 2001, was also found guilty of nineteen (out of twenty-eight) felony charges filed against him during the financial collapse of the corporation. Just to name a few, the courts found Skilling guilty of one count of conspiracy, one count of insider trading, five counts of making false statements and presentations to securities analysts and twelve counts of securities fraud.

42

Lastly, Enron's former Chief Financial Officer, Andrew S. Fastow, played a key role in hiding the corporation's massive losses through the mark-to-market and creative accounting practices. On October 31, 2002, Fastow was found guilty of seventy-eight counts of conspiracy, money laundering and fraud. In exchange for his testimony against other Enron top executives, Andrew Fastow agreed to serve a ten-year prison term. Kenneth Lay and Jeffrey Skilling faced up to 185 years in prison for their fraudulent activities and conspiracy at Enron. Lay, however, died of a heart attack before his sentence could be imposed.

49

There are many lessons to remember from the story of Enron's rise, prominence, and financial collapse. Although some people feel it is an account of justified achievement, growth, innovation, and creativity, most agree it is an unfortunate (but true) testimony of human greed, ambition, competitive deceit, and arrogance. Enron's story shows that the company's Code of Ethics didn't really mean anything because it was not applied equally to everyone in the corporation. There must be a genuine and strong commitment from top management to reinforce and support the principles and values that are set forth in a corporate Code of Ethics. Further, funds should be made available in each corporate budget to conduct ethics training (and possibly hire ethics officers) to communicate, implement, and integrate the ethical behavior into the firm's culture.

58

11. According to the author, all of the following are positive effects of competition EXCEPT:

    a. more educated workforce
    b. better ways to satisfy customers
    c. better quality products
    d. lowest possible price
    e. improves the search for new technologies

12. In Line 12, what does *deficit* mean?

    a. expenditure
    b. subterfuge
    c. impairment
    d. deficiency
    e. disadvantage

13. According to the author of the passage, which of the following is NOT a reason for Enron's bankruptcy?

    a. Irregular accounting procedures
    b. Unethical foreign investments
    c. Extravagant executive expenses
    d. Tax evasion
    e. Bank fraud

14. In Line 34, what does *audit* mean?

    a. government
    b. examination
    c. repercussion
    d. regulatory
    e. seizure

15. According to the author, which of the following best conveys the value of a corporation's Code of Ethics?

    a. It assures Wall Street investors of a firm's mission and goals
    b. It attracts the right type of employee at all levels of the organization
    c. It is only valuable if top managers support and reinforce its principles
    d. It is an essential public relations tool
    e. It has no intrinsic value

16. What is the tone of the passage?

    a. apathetic
    b. vainglorious
    c. dejected
    d. incredulous
    e. objective

17. Which of the following is the best title for the passage?

    a. The Criminal Consequences of Enron
    b. How Top Enron Managers Betrayed Their Corporate Code of Ethics
    c. How Enron Fell from Grace
    d. Fraud at Enron: The New Corporate Culture
    e. Enron: The Aftermath

Passage 3.

In 2005, scientists at Yale University were awarded a patent for "GeneTropy," a home-based DNA analysis kit. The practical implications of the kit are enormous to law enforcement groups, as GeneTropy makes a positive DNA match in just thirty minutes, compared to the minimal three-week period required by previous testing methodologies. Since GeneTropy's introduction, federal, state and local law enforcement agencies have used the test to solve over 400 rapes, 120 assaults and 6,100 burglaries. In Illinois, the test has also been used to reverse the wrongful convictions of eleven murderers, including three on Death Row.

7

The burgeoning market for home-based paternity testing offers another revenue stream for GeneTropy that its developers are eager to explore. During their initial promotional work, they discovered that traditional lab-based tests cost over $650 and offer results in three weeks. Of the five accredited labs in the United States, backlogs are usually so severe that the turnaround time can be five weeks or longer. In contrast, GeneTropy costs just $100, provides reliable results in 24 hours, and can be used in the privacy of a buyer's home. The developers' primary goal for 2010 is to get FDA approval for the over-the-counter distribution of the test. From a societal perspective, the potential financial and psychological benefits to families in America are too important to ignore.

15

18. What is the main point of the passage?

    a. To convince customers of traditional DNA labs to use GeneTropy as a lower cost option
    b. To encourage families to have paternity tests run on their children
    c. To discuss the low cost and fast speed of GeneTropy's DNA analysis kit
    d. To explain what GeneTropy can offer law enforcement groups
    e. To demonstrate Yale's financial interest in GeneTropy technology

19. According to the author, what is GeneTrophy's main advantage to law enforcement?

    a.   small sample size
    b.   low cost
    c.   fast results
    d.   reliability
    e.   FDA approved

20. In line 8, what does *burgeoning* mean?

    a.   unexpected
    b.   lucrative
    c.   sophisticated
    d.   expanding
    e.   consumer

21. According to the author, law enforcement agencies have used GeneTropy to solve all of the following crimes EXCEPT:

    a.   forgery
    b.   rape
    c.   murder
    d.   burglary
    e.   assault

22. For paternity tests, which of the following is NOT a benefit provided by GeneTrophy?

    a.   reliable
    b.   low cost
    c.   privacy
    d.   over-the-counter access
    e.   fast results

23. The author's attitude toward GeneTrophy can be best described as?

    a.   neutral
    b.   cynical
    c.   envious
    d.   enthusiastic
    e.   laconic

Passage 4.

In his article "Surfing The Mobile Wave," David Geer notes that business people have an insatiable appetite for technology that enables them to remain in touch on the go. This increased demand for mobility imposed by the organizations' own internal customers has motivated businesses to deploy more personal devices and mobile technologies than they initially anticipated. Consumers, along with corporations, acquire mobile and hand-held devices because they offer a variety of software applications, Internet and e-mail access, instant messaging, voice calls, and networking features that are conveniently accessible in a small, portable package.

7

The biggest reason, however, for such explosive growth in mobile technologies is the potential cost savings for the companies that use them. Advanced mobile and wireless devices allow firms to communicate independently of their physical locations. In addition, by 2015, wireless technology is forecasted to outperform wired networks due to its preferable cost, reliability, and functionality. Despite their convenience, flexibility, and cost-effectiveness, however, mobile technologies and devices pose ever-changing security challenges for a corporation's top management to ensure the integrity, privacy, confidentiality, reliability, and security of their corporate data.

15

The two main issues related to mobile devices are the storage of sensitive corporate information and the means of accessing the company's networks. Mobile devices provide remote access to a company's data, which provides tremendous flexibility to their users. This flexibility, however, leaves the company's networks and data vulnerable to security breaches and viruses. Furthermore, many companies are struggling to find ways to protect the increasing amount of sensitive information that is stored in laptops, PDAs, BlackBerries, cell phones, USB drives, and other portable devices, which can be easily stolen, lost, or carried away due to their small size. Although many companies have policies against storing sensitive company information on mobile devices, many users keep corporate data on them. Additionally, even though most devices offer password protection, most hackers can easily bypass these controls and access sensitive personal or business data.

25

Although laptops and mobile devices offer many advantages, when one is lost, the subsequent costs extend far beyond the physical replacement of the unit. In many cases, the greatest threat is the loss of sensitive or proprietary data that has been stored on the device. While studies have shown that the theft of computers containing sensitive data is associated with only a small percentage of identity theft, the possible liability associated with losing confidential information is significant. Additionally, the majority of U.S. states now require that businesses notify those who might be at risk for fraud, which brings unwanted negative publicity.

32

Preventing the loss of these devices has been much more difficult than securing traditional workstation computers. Laptops, PDA's, smart phones, and USB memory sticks are smaller and extremely portable, which enables employees to transfer sensitive information from secured networks to the device and remove it from the company premises. Although some companies may not allow CD burners at their workstation computers, laptops, PDAs, and USB drives are as commonplace as house keys. Even more troubling, when cheap USB memory devices are missing, employees may not even report it.

39

Unfortunately, the loss of these devices is all too common. Last year, about 750,000 laptops were stolen; about 97% of stolen PC's are never recovered. Every month, thousands of mobile phones are also stolen. If they are smart phones, they could contain private information like computer files and email messages, which could spark an unwanted leak of sensitive company information. According to a survey performed by the Yankee Group in 2005, 37 percent of respondents attributed the disclosure of company information to USB drives.

46

In a survey last year, the Computer Security Institute of the Federal Bureau of Investigation reported that 75% of respondents experienced laptop and mobile device theft, which was more than any other type of attack or misuse, including denial of service attacks, telecommunications fraud, unauthorized access of information, viruses, financial fraud, insider abuse of net access, system penetration, sabotage, theft of proprietary information, abuse of a wireless network, website defacement, and misuse of a public web application.

52

According to a survey performed by the Ponemon Institute, 81 percent of information security professionals reported that their companies had experienced the loss of one or more laptops containing sensitive information. The study also reported that hand-held devices and laptops were the storage devices that posed the greatest risk of data loss, followed by USB memory sticks. Sensitive information could include customer data, employee records, vendor information, intellectual property (such as product or research data, corporate plans, and strategies), and even the secret personal correspondence of key employees, which might make them vulnerable to blackmail.

60

Currently, there are numerous products and services to recover missing or stolen devices. Companies like SmartProtec provide software that can trace stolen property and return it to its rightful owner. Mr. Shively, an inventory manager for a company that processes medical records, recently installed SmartProtec software on more than 900 computers that are used by employees who travel between hospitals to scan patient records. If any of these computers are stolen, Mr. Shively simply has to call a hotline; the next time that laptop is connected to the internet, it will automatically send a message to the servers at SmartProtec headquarters that identifies its location. Immediately afterwards, the same information is forwarded to the police, who can retrieve the stolen laptop.

69

SmartProtec provides a similar service for cell phones, which allows users to register their devices. This simple step makes it dangerous for thieves to possess or re-sell stolen items. SmartProtec works with the police and other authorities to recover stolen devices, and even offers rewards to those who help find them. The serial numbers of all devices are stored in a SmartProtec database, so there is no need for the owner to write it on a piece of paper and worry about losing it. The moment the device is lost or stolen, the owner must immediately change its status from "In Possession" to "Lost" or "Stolen." When police recover a stolen item, or somebody comes across a lost device, SmartProtec allows them to contact the owner through the serial number, without disclosing any personal information. Moreover, SmartProtec collaborates with FedEx to deliver the recovered device directly to the owner's doorstep.

79

Executives must keep these security services in their proper perspective. Although SmartProtec can trace stolen property and return it safely to its rightful owner, no amount of technology can substitute completely for the actions of people. Ultimately, security is only as good as each company's individual policies.

83

24. By 2015, what technological change do industry experts expect?

    a.   Corporations will no longer allow employees to store sensitive data on mobile devices
    b.   SmartProtec will capture more than eighty-percent of the wireless security market
    c.   The theft of mobile devices will spark a corresponding rise in identity theft
    d.   Due to problems associated with theft, USB memory devices will be prohibited at most major corporations
    e.   Wireless technology will outperform wired networks

25. According to the passage, what percentage of stolen laptops is recovered?

    a.   3%
    b.   37%
    c.   75%
    d.   81%
    e.   97%

26. The passage mentions all of the following mobile devices EXCEPT:

    a.   Smart phones
    b.   USB drives
    c.   BlackBerries
    d.   Memory sticks
    e.   Portable microchips

27. In Line 43, what does *sensitive* mean?

    a.   Easily hurt
    b.   Classified
    c.   Clandestine
    d.   Delicate
    e.   Reactionary

28. Which organization conducted a survey to determine how sensitive company information was erroneously disclosed?

    a.   Yankee Group
    b.   Federal Bureau of Investigation
    c.   Ponemon Institut
    d.   SmartProtec
    e.   Computer Security Institute

29. In the survey conducted by the Ponemon Institute, which of the following is NOT mentioned as a type of record kept on corporate computers?

    a.   Vendor information
    b.   Corporate strategies
    c.   Secret personal correspondence
    d.   Health and medical records
    e.   Employee records

30. In which scenario would the SmartProtec system NOT be helpful?

    a.   The thief takes the laptop outside the United States
    b.   The owner forgets the hotline number
    c.   The thief does not attempt to log onto the Internet
    d.   The laptop is dropped
    e.   The laptop is sold to a pawn shop

31. In line 72, what does *serial* mean?

    a.   identifying
    b.   in order
    c.   repetitive
    d.   rank
    e.   production

32. Which of the following best conveys the author's attitude about the security of mobile devices?

    a.   There is no realistic way to secure them.
    b.   The risks are minimal compared to the benefits these devices offer.
    c.   Portable storage devices should be banned at most companies to prevent security risks.
    d.   Their security depends on each company's policies.
    e.   A system like SmartProtec provides adequate protection for most users' needs.

Answer Key to Reading Comprehension Questions

1. Choice D is correct. The other choices are either too broad or narrow in scope.

2. Choice E is correct. In this context, *arena* is a forum, or opportunity to exchange ideas.

3. Choice C is correct. All of the other answer choices are mentioned in the passage.

4. Choice C is correct. The answer is presented in Lines 13 – 15.

5. Choice D is correct. The answer is presented in Lines 16 – 21.

6. Choice D is correct. The answer is presented in Line 28.

7. Choice E is correct. The answer is presented in Lines 30 – 31.

8. Choice A is correct. The answer is presented in the sixth paragraph, Lines 37 – 46.

9. Choice C is correct. In this context, a *pet issue* is a special interest.

10. Choice C is correct. The answer is presented in the final sentence of the passage.

11. Choice A is correct. All of the other choices are mentioned in the first paragraph of Passage A.

12. Choice D is correct. In this context, *deficit* means deficiency.

13. Choice D is correct. All of the other choices are mentioned in Passage A (Lines 15 – 17 and Lines 31 – 35).

14. Choice B is correct. In this *context*, audit means examination.

15. Choice C is correct. The author explains his position in Lines 53 – 54.

16. Choice E is correct. The author is objective in tone.

17. Choice B is correct. The other choices are either too broad or too narrow in scope.

18. Choice C is correct. The other answer choices are either too broad or too narrow in scope.

19. Choice C is correct. In Line 3, the author cites the fast speed of the test, which is the greatest advantage for law enforcement applications.

20. Choice D is correct. In this context, *burgeoning* means expanding.

21. Choice A is correct. The passage mentions all of the other crimes in the first paragraph.

22. Choice D is correct. The FDA has not yet approved the test for over-the-counter sales.

23. Choice D is correct. The final statement in the passage confirms the author's enthusiasm about GeneTropy.

24. Choice E is correct. The answer is in Line 10.

25. Choice A is correct. On Line 41, the author reports that 97% of stolen laptops are NOT recovered.

26. Choice E is correct. All of the other devices are mentioned in the passage.

27. Choice B is correct. In this context, *sensitive* means classified.

28. Choice A is correct. The answer is in Line 44.

29. Choice D is correct. The other choices are mentioned in Lines 56 – 59.

30. Choice C is correct. According to Lines 65 – 66, the laptop can only be traced if the thief logs onto the Internet, when its location can be determined from its IP number. If the thief does not log onto the Internet, the unit cannot be traced.

31. Choice A is correct. The *serial* number corresponds with the ownership certificate, which identifies the registered user of the laptop.

32. Choice D is correct. The author states this conclusion in the final sentence of the passage.

Chapter 6: Analytical Writing Assessment

The Analytical Writing Assessment requires students to write two essays within 75 minutes:

Perspective on an Issue, which asks candidates to take a position on a social issue (30 minutes)

Analysis of an Argument, which asks candidates to evaluate an argument or critique a line of reasoning (30 minutes)

On the day of the test, you will write your analyses before you tackle the other sections of the GRE. After you turn in your exam, two separate graders will read your essays and assign them a score between 1 and 6 (1 is the lowest score, while 6 is the highest).

The people who grade your essay do not care which position you take, which means that there is no "right" or "wrong" answer to the essay prompts. Instead, the graders will judge your essay for clarity, consistency, organization and the use of examples. A terrific analysis will also have an engaging opening, a good flow of ideas, smooth transitions between paragraphs, and a short (but relevant) conclusion. The following criteria define each score:

Outstanding (6): a cohesive, well-supported discussion of the issue, with insightful reasoning and/or persuasive examples. Excellent writing style, including varied sentence structure, precise vocabulary and superior grammar.

Good / Solid (5): an effective, well-organized essay with appropriate examples. Contains occasional lapses in quality.

Adequate (4): presents a competent discussion of the issue/argument. Expresses ideas clearly with adequate organization. May lack sentence variety and include some grammatical flaws.

Limited / Below Average (3): inadequate essay with limited organization and inadequate examples to support the position. Displays flaws in grammar and/or mechanics.

Flawed / Disappointing (2): Vague essay with limited or inconsistent examples to support the position. Contains errors in grammar, mechanics, vocabulary and word choice.

Poor / Deficient (1): Deficient in basic writing skills; poor analysis of the issue. The essay is unfocused and disorganized, with serious errors in language and sentence structure.

Unable to Score (0): Essay is off-topic or incomprehensible

Because of the short timeframe, the graders do not expect perfection. They understand that your essay will be a first draft that you wrote written under fairly stressful conditions. What, then, is the purpose of the Analytical Writing Assessment? It is your chance to demonstrate:

  a.   excellent reasoning skills
  b.   superior writing skills
  c.   the ability to quickly organize your thoughts
  d.   the ability to produce a coherent essay in the required timeframe

Here are the directions for the **Perspective on an Issue**:

Directions: Analyze and present your point of view on the issue described below. There is no "right" point of view. In developing your analysis, you should consider the issue from a number of different viewpoints. Read the statement below and the directions that follow it.

The **Analysis of an Argument** topic gives these directions:

Directions : Provide a critique of the argument below. Focus on one (or all) of the following, depending upon your opinion of the argument: questionable assumptions underlying the reasoning, alternative explanations or evidence that would weaken the reasoning or additional information that would support or weaken the argument. Read the statement below and the directions that follow it.

For each analysis, you will have 30 minutes to make a written case. By design, the topics chosen by the test writers do not require any knowledge of a specific academic area. Instead, the prompts are usually quotations about current events or issues that we all think differently about. After the quote, you will be asked to take a side on the issue and support your position with concrete examples from your reading, studies, experiences, or observations. To receive a top score, you must write an essay that is clear, persuasive, well organized, and supported by relevant examples.

Strategy 1. For the first five minutes, decide which position you want to take on the issue. Then, write a short outline of what you plan to say, with concrete examples to prove each point. Ideally, you should know what you want to say and how you want to say it *before* you start writing the actual essay.

In these precious first minutes, don't waste time trying to decide which side to take. In every case, the alternatives will be evenly matched, with no "right" or "wrong" choice. Keep in mind the grading criteria: you will be evaluated strictly by how well you support your choice with reasoning and evidence.

Regardless of your feelings about the topic, you should *pick the side for which you can build the strongest case in 25 minutes*. In a perfect world, you would have three hours to research the topic on the Internet and secure enough information to support either side. Unfortunately, you will be working within an unusually abbreviated timeframe, which means that you must make the most of the examples and ideas that come into your head during the first five minutes.

Strategy 2. Because of the short time limit, you should limit yourself to two or three examples to support your position. If you try to write include additional examples, you may not have enough time to write a good introduction and conclusion.

Surprisingly, many students struggle when they try to find "evidence" for their essays. They think that they need to possess an armload of facts and figures to support their position. From our perspective, persuasive evidence can come from any part of your life, including your own personal experiences. In fact, the BEST essays tend to be well-balanced passages that draw evidence from two or three different sources.

Example: Suppose that your essay prompt asked you to take a position on the statement, "Most people are sheep; they simply follow the crowd." Although this is a harsh (and somewhat cynical) viewpoint, let's build a case for the adversarial position: people are free thinkers who create meaningful change.

Your evidence could come from three areas:

History: Pick someone who showed extraordinary leadership under difficult circumstances. The ideal candidate is someone who championed an unpopular viewpoint, such as Abraham Lincoln, who decided to free the slaves.

Literature: Choose a hero who challenged authority (or traditional thinking), such as the Wright brothers, who refused to believe that they couldn't fly.

Personal Anecdote: Choose a friend or family member who had the courage to champion an important cause. Explain why this person is an inspiration to you.

These three examples are enough to build a compelling GRE essay.

Strategy 3. When drafting your outline, jot down one or two points that support the *opposite* position. Ideally, you will include these thoughts in the introduction or conclusion of your essay, both to acknowledge the alternative viewpoint and to reinforce why you dispute it.

This is a risky strategy, however, if you overdo it; your goal is not to confuse the reader, but to convince him/her that you came to your conclusion after careful and intelligent deliberation. If handled correctly, this technique enhances your credibility and makes the resulting essay even stronger.

Example: This is a sample opening for an essay in which the author disputes the contention that all people are sheep. She effectively uses the opposing argument to launch her discussion of three people who were political activists during trying times.

Throughout history, few people have dared to resist the status quo. Rather than question their nation's laws or politics, they placed complete trust in their elected leaders to make well-reasoned decisions on their behalf. Thankfully, each generation also brings a new set of "rebels," such as Rosa Parks, Dr. Martin Luther King Jr., and Jane Roe, who challenged the validity of misguided "cultural norms," such as slavery, racial segregation and illegal abortion. These brazen activists, who risked their freedom, livelihood, and reputations to challenge the Constitution, provide an inspiring example of man's determination to create a fairer and more equitable government.

This is a powerful opening to an essay that discussed the lives of Rosa Parks, Martin Luther King, Jr. and Jane Roe (from the landmark legal case, Roe Vs. Wade). By acknowledging the rarity of their achievements, and the uphill battle they faced to challenge the cultural norm, the author convinced the reader in the first paragraph that they were rare and special people. Not surprisingly, the author ended the essay with a similar call to advocacy, by encouraging the reader to defend and protect the rights that each of these pioneers held dear.

Strategy 4. Immediately after you finish your outline, you must write an opening statement that reveals your position on the topic. Additionally, your opening must be creative enough to interest and entice the reader.

In your introduction, get to the point immediately. If the essay prompt presents a question, your first few sentences should provide your answer. Likewise, if the prompt asks you to choose one side or another, you should state your choice clearly and effectively. Don't waste any time or space rehashing the scenario and the alternatives. Offer an interpretation in light of the stated criteria. It's up to you to indicate why certain facts are positive or negative. The best opening statements are creative, rather than dry. Consider:

a.   using an short anecdote
b.   asking a question
c.   citing a quotation
d.   defining a word or idea

Once again, no one expects perfection. It's perfectly fine to open your essay in one of the following ways:

"A Greek philosopher once claimed that "nature abhors a vacuum," but my experiences as a chemistry student suggest otherwise."

"As a child, I defined success in monetary terms. As an adult, I am more appreciative of its personal and emotional components."

"What is the true cost of freedom? Whatever is necessary to protect the cherished rights in the United States Constitution."

All three of these options state the writer's position and launch the essay in the desired direction.

Strategy 5. After your introductory paragraph, you should provide at least two or three examples to support your position. Restrict each discussion to a separate paragraph, making sure to explain how each example supports the overall theme of the essay. The better organized your essay, the more persuasive it will be.

Present your examples in *their relative order of importance*; you want to win over your audience as quickly as possible by presenting your strongest material first. Make the most of your evidence and examples. Each paragraph should explain:

The actual evidence or example
How the person, situation or data support your position

Strategy 6. Make sure that your essay flows in a clear and logical manner. Develop good transitional sentences between paragraphs that guide the reader from one point to another. For GRE essays, your primary transitions will be from one example (or piece of evidence) to another.

Let's assume that you are writing the essay about the political advocacy of Rosa Parks, Dr. Martin Luther King, Jr. and Jane Roe. Let's also assume that you want to discuss them in that order. For convenience, we have copied the introductory paragraph below:

Throughout history, few people have dared to resist the status quo. Rather than question their nation's laws or politics, they placed complete trust in their elected leaders to make well-reasoned decisions on their behalf. Thankfully, each generation also brings a new set of "rebels," such as Rosa Parks, Dr. Martin Luther King Jr., and Jane Roe, who challenged the validity of misguided "cultural norms," such as slavery, racial segregation and illegal abortion. These brazen activists, who risked their freedom, livelihood, and reputations to challenge the Constitution, provide an inspiring example of man's determination to create a fairer and more equitable government.

Example 1: For the remainder of the essay, you could use a ***chronological technique*** to make a logical transition between paragraphs:

Paragraph 2. *When Rosa Parks refused to give up her seat on the bus in 1955, she launched the revolution that eventually became known as the Civil Rights Movement.*

Paragraph 3. *Inspired by the bravery of Ms. Parks, Dr. Martin Luther King Jr. became an impassioned spokesman on behalf of racial equality in all fifty states.*

Paragraph 4. *In 1973, a frightened single mother in Texas named Jane Roe challenged the nation's longstanding laws against reproductive freedom.*

Example 2: Alternatively, you could use a more ***creative approach*** that highlights each person's commitment to equality:

Paragraph 2. *Rosa Parks became the first pioneer in the Civil Rights Movement when she refused to give up her seat on a bus to a white man in 1955.*

Paragraph 3. *To spread his belief in an integrated nation, Dr. Martin Luther King, Jr. made impassioned speeches to an enraptured public in all fifty states.*

Paragraph 4. *Unlike Ms. Parks and Dr. King, who became famous for their advocacy, the pioneer for women's reproductive rights was simply known as Jane Roe.*

There are dozens of ways to structure this essay in a logical and compelling way. Considering the short time that you will have to write the essay, we recommend that you keep your transitions brief and simple. Try different types of transitions for this essay; see which ones work best for you.

Strategy 7. On the Analytical Writing Section of the GRE, the graders will examine your proficiency in all aspects of written English. Accordingly, you must avoid common errors in spelling, grammar and writing mechanics. If you are rusty in this area, review Appendix 5 in this publication, which provides a basic grammar review for the GRE.

Also take the time to review the material in Appendix 6, which reveals the most common errors in word choice that students make in their essays, including:

a. Words and phrases that are <u>always wrong</u>, such as *alot, anyways, enthuse* and *being that*.

b. Commonly confused words and phrases, such as *already vs. all ready, farther vs. further, fewer vs. less,* and *whether vs. if*.

c. Commonly confused verbs, such as *affect vs. effect, lay vs. lie,* and *leave vs. let*.

d. Common idiomatic mistakes, such as *conform with, different than, identical to,* and *independent from*.

Many students believe they are "home free" on these issues because the GRE does not include a formal section on grammar. Nothing could be further from the truth. The graders will assess your mastery of these topics – and the quality of your vocabulary – by the content of your essays. Over the years, we've seen several students submit essays that were strong, logical, and persuasive – but filled with idiomatic mistakes and errors in word choice. They did not obtain a top score. By taking the time to review these lists, you can avoid the most common (and preventable) mistakes.

Strategy 8. Adopt the appropriate tone. Write persuasively, but resist the urge to sound pompous or preachy. Choose simple words and syntax that reflect your true personality. Remember, your goal is to be clear, well organized and persuasive. For this essay, you need to achieve a healthy balance between style and substance.

What do we mean by *style*? Keep the essay lively and interesting by using sufficient details and descriptive phrases. Use the active voice. Vary your sentence pattern and length; make every word count.

Strategy 9. After you present your final example, you should reinforce your position in a short, one-paragraph conclusion. Keep an eye on the clock while you are writing the essay. If you are short on time when you reach the final paragraph, use a short and simple ending to reiterate your position and why you feel that way. Do NOT, under any circumstances, omit the ending, because it will suggest that you are not able to organize and manage your time. Here are two short (and terrific) ways to end an essay:

Example 1: Reiterate the main point and explain its relevance:

Thanks to the bravery and tenacity of Rosa Parks, Dr. Martin Luther King, Jr. and Jane Roe, U.S. citizens enjoy many rights and privileges that would not otherwise be possible. Their valiant efforts are the cornerstone of American democracy.

Example 2: Relate the point of the essay to your own life:

The selfless efforts of Rosa Parks, Dr. Martin Luther King, Jr. and Jane Roe demonstrate the power of a single person to change the world in a meaningful way. On a personal level, they have inspired my own commitment to volunteerism.

Strategy 10. The most common question about GRE essays is "How long should they be?" Without knowing the topic at hand (or the strength of your examples), we hesitate to suggest an absolute word limit. From our experience, however, essays that earn scores of 5 and 6 are usually at least 250 to 400 words long. Shorter essays rarely have the number (or quality) of examples that the graders expect to see.

On the other hand, essays over 500 words are generally too ambitious to be completed successfully in such a short period of time. The graders are looking for a successful balance of quality and quantity in your essay; it is pointless to include too many details if it requires you to sacrifice organization and style.

Our best advice is to include:

1. an introductory paragraph that clearly states your position
2. two or three relevant examples (one paragraph each)
3. one closing paragraph, with a persuasive conclusion

If this seems like a simplistic approach, remember your timeframe. Assuming that you take 5 minutes to choose your position and outline the essay, you will only have 20 minutes to write it. Three well-developed paragraphs, which contain independent pieces of evidence, are more than enough to support your thesis. If you lead into them with a creative opening, and conclude with a persuasive ending, you will fulfill the graders' expectations.

Strategy 11. If you encounter a topic that you cannot discuss intelligently, or for which you have no relevant examples, try to relate the topic to your own life. The sample essay below represents exactly that situation. The writer was a graduate of a large public high school in San Francisco. He did not know anyone who had been home-schooled, nor was he particularly comfortable citing facts or statistics on the subject. Instead, he explained why he felt that attending a large high school was the best choice for *him*. The resulting essay, which includes several relevant details and evidence, was well written and memorable. It is honest, easy to read and includes great quotes in the first and last paragraphs. From our perspective, it is an incredible example of what you can write in 25 minutes.

Example 1: Perspective on an Issue:

Many people believe that children who are home schooled by their parents will be more productive and happier than children who attend school in a traditional classroom. But others assert that the close supervision and social dynamics of a classroom are necessary to ensure productivity and to develop superior interpersonal skills.

Which argument do you find more compelling, the case for home schooling or the opposing viewpoint? Explain your viewpoint using relevant examples drawn from your own experience, observations or reading.

Assignment: Which argument do you find more compelling: the case for home schooling or the opposing viewpoint? Explain your position using relevant reasons or examples from your own experiences, observations, or reading.

The Outline:

Position: attending school is better

Introduction: President's Clinton's quote: Education is more than what we learn in books
Home schooling benefits (customization, no peer pressure, self-paced learning) do not outweigh disadvantages

Benefits of school:

1. Breadth of classes / explore & discover new talents

2. Teachers are experts in specific areas: can handle off-beat and intricate questions

3. Unbiased evaluation of performance

4. Social skills and outside groups provide source for maturity and development. Learn how to interact w/ different types of people. Excellent preparation for college and beyond

Conclusion: Recent stats about job change. Need flexibility. People skills. Ability to work on high performance teams. We get this from school

The Essay (received two scores of 6)

During his commencement address at Harvard University, former President Bill Clinton noted that education was far more than what students learn from books; it is

63

the accumulation of every academic, personal, cultural and recreational experience that we bring into our lives. Each interaction and activity that we choose to pursue has the power to open our minds to new ideas and perspectives, which eventually broaden our world. From my own experiences at a large metropolitan high school, and those of other students in different learning environments, I am convinced that the optimal place for education is in the classroom, rather than my own home.

Over time, I have considered the merits of several arguments in favor of home schooling. For non-traditional students, particularly those with learning disabilities, it provides an ambient learning environment that is free of social expectations and peer pressure. Home schooling enthusiasts also cite the benefits of self-paced learning, in which the parent and child can create a lesson plan that suits the student's individual needs. But, for me, the drawbacks of a home-based education far outweigh its advantages.

Attending a traditional high school offers numerous academic, social and recreational benefits that few parents can give their children. At Davis High School, I built a challenging curriculum that included 10 Advanced Placement courses in 5 academic areas. My teachers were all national experts in their fields, who were well prepared to answer unusual and intricate questions. They could also provide an objective assessment of my performance, compared to the thousands of other students they had taught in their distinguished careers.

Although my parents are well educated, their mastery of quantitative subjects like math and science does not compare to that of my teachers, Dr. Bennett and Mr. Gray. As an aspiring engineer, I was honored to reap the benefits of such an impressive level of instruction in the classroom and the lab. Without the generosity and support of Davis's faculty, I would not have had the confidence to pursue such a rigorous major.

Davis High School also offered the opportunity for me to explore my talents in art, music, athletics and debate. In a home-schooling environment, I would have shied away from these challenges, which were originally quite intimidating. By flexing my wings in the company of my fellow students, I not only uncovered a few unexpected talents, but made several close friends in the process. In fact, these connections with my teachers and fellow students were probably the greatest blessing that I reaped from attending school. By working with other students on class projects, team sports, and numerous charitable endeavors, I learned that success is rarely a solitary event; great things happen when a group of people combines their energy in support of a common goal.

In 2004, Jack Welch, the retired CEO of GE, noted that most college graduates will change jobs 8 times in their careers. Accordingly, their greatest assets are flexibility and interpersonal skills, which enable them to quickly adapt to new people, places and situations. I could not learn these skills sitting at the kitchen table listening to a history lecture from my mother. I can only achieve my personal best by going to school, engaging with others, and sampling the world of opportunities that are available to me, if I am only willing to ask.

Why is this essay so good? The author relates every paragraph back to his position that traditional schooling is best. Citing his many achievements at Davis High School, he makes a compelling argument that he would not have received as broad and satisfying an education at home. Amazingly, the author also acknowledged the alternative viewpoint in a respectful and intelligent manner. His level of insight, particularly regarding Jack Welch's comments on career strengths, is highly unusual for a college senior.

Analysis of an Argument

Be prepared to apply additional strategies for the Analysis of an Argument prompt, in which the author is trying to convince you of something (his conclusion) by citing specific evidence. Your job is to evaluate the writer's assumptions - and how he makes the leap from evidence to conclusion.

The question stem will usually ask you to evaluate the strength of the argument and to suggest possible ways to improve it. Other times, the question will take the opposite approach and ask you why the argument is not persuasive - and to supply additional information that will weaken it. Either way, your objective is to:

a. analyze the argument
b. evaluate its use of evidence
c. explain how a different approach (or more information) would strengthen or weaken the argument

Strategy 12. Take the argument apart quickly and methodically. First, identify the conclusion. Then, look at the evidence that the author uses to support it. Restate it in your own words.

Evaluate the *persuasiveness* of the argument. Does the evidence support it? Does it use the correct evidence in an effective manner - or are there flaws in the logic and unwarranted assumptions? Determine the additional evidence or information you would need to increase the validity of the argument. Your job is to identify the issue, take a side, and explain the merits and drawbacks of the author's position.

Strategy 13. Next, follow the same approach that you used for the Analysis of an Issue to outline and write your essay. Use scrap paper to make a rudimentary outline, including the points you want to make in each paragraph.

Strategy 14. When you write your essay, get to the point immediately. Your first paragraph should offer your assessment of the argument and its reasoning. Then, you should discuss the additional evidence that would make the argument more persuasive. Always provide evidence for your claims; do not make assertions that you cannot support. To whatever extent possible, write in a calm and objective way; by adopting a professional tone, you will gain credibility with your reader.

Here is an excellent example of an Analysis of an Argument

Example 2: Analysis of an Argument

Conjugal visits should not be discontinued in prisons that house dangerous felons, including death row inmates. Those convicted of serious crimes should serve their prison sentences, but they should not be denied their right to basic human contact. Most violent criminals are comforted by touch and need to reinforce their positive bonds with their spouses and families. To deny them this basic human right is to deprive prisoners of a harmless outlet for their aggression and make them more dangerous.

Assignment: Explain how logical and persuasive you find this argument. When you present your viewpoint, analyze the argument's line of reasoning and use of evidence. Also, explain what, if anything, would make the argument more convincing or help you to evaluate its conclusion.

The Outline:

1. I **disagree** with the author's conclusion that convicted felons deserve the right to conjugal visits.

2. **His arguments**:

a) all humans need touch,, which makes them less aggressive
b) to deprive them of touch would make them more dangerous
c) prisoners retain these rights while they are incarcerated

3. **My concerns**:

a) prisoners forfeit their rights upon conviction
b) there is no proof that conjugal visits make prisoners less aggressive
c) the high recidivism rate suggests that these programs do not work

4. **Additional evidence** that is needed:

a) that positive relationships reduce violent crime
b) that death row inmates deserve any sort of rights

The Analysis (received two scores of 6)

The author concludes that violent prisoners should be allowed to have conjugal visits to satisfy their needs for basic human contact. His argument is that all people, including violent felons, are comforted by touch and will be less aggressive if they can satisfy their sexual needs. Furthermore, the author suggests that these benefits should extend to death row inmates, although they have no hope for rehabilitation or release.

I detect two unwarranted assumptions in the author's reasoning. First, he assumes that convicted criminals retain their right to intimate contact while they are incarcerated. I vehemently disagree. Criminals forfeit this civil liberty when they are sentenced to prison, along with their right to move freely in society. From a social and physical perspective, an inmate's separation from his friends, family, and loved ones is an integral part of his punishment. To restore it arbitrarily would defeat the entire purpose of his prison sentence.

The author also presumes that providing an inmate with a "harmless outlet" for the release of aggression will make him less violent. Sadly, anecdotal evidence does not support this assumption. With a recidivism rate of almost 60%, our prisons are filled with repeat offenders who could not succeed in society after their release. Their initial prison sentences, which included conjugal visits, left them as angry and violent as they were before.

The author could strengthen his argument by providing quantitative evidence that people who form positive intimate relationships are less likely to commit violent crimes. Alternatively, he could provide statistical evidence to prove that inmates who enjoy conjugal visits are more likely to be successfully rehabilitated than those who do not. Finally, he must offer a valid argument to support his contention that death row inmates, who are the most violent and dangerous criminals of all, deserve this sort of benefit. Without this evidence, the author's conclusion is difficult to support.

This essay, although short, is well-written and conceived. The first paragraphs outline the argument effectively and note the inconsistency between the conclusion and the evidence; the final paragraph offers compelling suggestions to improve the argument. From a mechanical perspective, the organization, sentence structure, and grammar are excellent (Score = 6).

Strategy 15.   Many students, in anticipation of the Analytical Writing Assessment, ask us to explain the "secret" of good writing. As far as we know, the only way to become a good writer is to write as much as possible, as often as possible. By doing so, you will find your voice and become comfortable putting pen to paper.

For the Analytical Writing Assessment, your task is simple - you must answer the question in an honest and concise manner. State your position clearly and back it up with facts and examples. That is all the graders expect.

If you stop to consider why the essays are required, it may put the assignment into the proper perspective. Graduate school will require a lot of writing, regardless of the profession you choose. Before a program admits you, the admissions committee wants to know that you are up to the task. The Analytical Writing Assessment will document your writing and organizational skills in a practical and unique way. For well-prepared candidates, the two essays are truly an opportunity to shine.

Chapter 7: Quantitative Section of the GRE™

The quantitative section of the GRE contains 28 multiple choice questions in a 45-minute timeframe. The 28 questions are divided among three types: Problem Solving, Data Interpretation, and Quantitative Comparisons.

The math topics on the GRE include arithmetic, basic algebra and geometry (no proofs). Trigonometry and calculus are NOT included. According to the ETS, the test writers carefully choose questions to place all students on a level playing field. To whatever extent possible, they try to eliminate biases that favor candidates with specific strengths and backgrounds.

From our perspective (after reviewing numerous versions of the GRE), the quantitative section is designed to test your ability to solve problems, rather than your mathematical knowledge. The questions lean heavily toward word problems and applying mathematical formulas in typical real-world applications, such as calculating:

- The interest on a loan
- The percentage drop of a stock price
- A salary increase (or decrease)
- Travel times and speeds
- Work schedules

Although the test writers vary their questions from year to year, certain topics tend to appear with similar frequency on the GRE. Recent exam questions fell into the following categories:

Ratios, Rates, Percentages	25%
Word Problems	25%
Number Properties	25%
Geometry	20%
Other	5%

Here's the great news for students; from our experience, nearly every test question has a simple solution and can be solved with a minimum of calculations. The trick is to correctly assess each question and apply the correct strategy.

In our introductory chapter, we recommended that you familiarize yourself with the instructions for each section of the exam beforehand, to avoid wasting time on them on the day of the test. This advice is particularly relevant for the quantitative section, which provides a wealth of reference information for you to use. Her are the instructions for the GRE math sections:

For Multiple Choice Questions:

Directions: This section contains two types of questions. You have 25 minutes to complete both types. For questions 1 – 12, solve each problem and decide which is the best of the choices given. Fill in the corresponding circle on the answer sheet. You may use any available space for scratch work.

For Quantitative Comparisons:

Each question has two quantities to be compared: one in Column A and one in Column B. Compare the quantities taking into consideration any other information given and choose:

Answer A - if the quantity in Column A is greater
Answer B - if the quantity in Column B is greater
Answer C - if the two quantities are equal
Answer D - if the relationship cannot be determined without further information.

Notes:
1. *The use of a calculator is permitted.*
2. *All numbers used are real numbers.*
3. *Figures that accompany problems in this test are intended to provide valuable information useful in solving the problems. They are drawn as accurately as possible EXCEPT when it is stated in a*

specific problem that the figure is not drawn to scale. All figures lie in a plane unless otherwise indicated.

4. Unless otherwise specified, the domain of any function f is assumed to be the set of all real numbers x for which f (x) is a real number.

Reference Information:

1. Circles. Area $= \pi r^2$, Circumference $= 2 \pi r$
2. Rectangles: Area = Length X Width
3. Right Triangles: Area = ½ (Base) (Height)
4. Cubes: Volume = Length x Width x Height
5. Cylinders: Volume $= \pi r^2 h$
6. Pythagorean Theorem: for right triangles $c^2 = a^2 + b^2$

Tips and Strategies:

The GRE covers the same mathematical, geometric and algebraic topics every time. Before you take the test, thoroughly review the following basic concepts in Appendix 7 (or in your own textbooks for these classes). Work on the areas in which you need improvement. Practice each question type until you are confident you can succeed.

Basic arithmetic	Factoring algebraic expressions
Number properties	Solving equations
Divisibility	Word problems
Fractions and decimals	Coordinate geometry
Percents	Lines and angles
Ratios, Proportions and Rates	Triangles
Mean, Median and Mode	Squares and rectangles
Possibility and probability	Circles
Exponents and radicals	Polygons
Algebraic expressions	Solids

Don't waste time memorizing any of the formulas relating to triangles, circles and other geometric shapes, because the GRE provides that information at the beginning of every quantitative section of the exam. Likewise, don't worry about making tons of difficult calculations, because basic calculators ARE allowed inside the test hall. Instead, focus on how you must USE the information and tools you are given to solve typical questions and problems. As you might expect, there are many tricks, traps and strategies to help guide your way.

Strategy 1. The problems in the quantitative section are presented in the order of difficulty. If math is an "issue" for you, or you think you will have problems completing the entire section, use this knowledge to your advantage. Slow down. Don't worry about getting to the final few problems. Instead, take your time and rack up as many "easy" points as you can on the first questions in the section. It would be a shame to get an easy problem wrong because you were rushing to the final section, where the points are significantly harder to acquire.

Strategy 2. All problems on the test are worth the same, regardless of their level of difficulty. If you have time to tackle any of the tougher problems (questions 18 and higher), be selective in which ones you try. Quickly review them to see if there is a type that you are particularly good at; if so, do that one before the others. Don't waste time on something complicated and intimidating. It's not worth any more points than the easier ones.

Strategy 3. For standard multiple choice questions, students have an advantage, because the correct answer is right in front of them. For these questions, elimination strategies are paramount. First, be aware that the GRE lists all answer choices in ascending order:

Example:

    a. 3
    b. 9
    c. 12
    d. 36
    e. 72

At first glance, this might not seem like particularly useful information. But let's put it into several contexts that reveal its hidden power. First, let's assume that these five answers were for a problem that asked you to calculate the amount of money that someone had left over after buying back-to-school supplies. Let's also assume that you reach this problem with only a few minutes left in the math section, but you think it's worth a shot.

If you are going to approach the problem by plugging the answer choices into an equation, start with the middle answer, which is 12. Why (other than that you hope it is the right answer)? Because even if 12 wrong, you will have narrowed your answer choices from 4 possibilities to 2.

If 12 is too large to be the right answer, you will automatically know that the correct answer will be either A or B. Likewise, if 12 is too small to be correct, you will know that the right answer to the problem is D or E. Even if you run out of time and wind up guessing, you have increased your odds of getting the right answer.

Strategy 4. Develop an overall strategy that will work for all types of quantitative problems, regardless of type or difficulty. Our tried-and-true system, which we will use throughout the remainder of this chapter:

1.   Read the question quickly and carefully.
2.   Identify what you are being asked.
3.   Eliminate all extraneous information.
4.   Organize your facts.
5.   Decide what calculations you need to perform.
6.   Do them in the correct order.
7.   Check your answer (including the units) to ensure that it makes sense.

Strategy 5. The drawback of multiple choice questions is that the test writers can usually anticipate the errors that you are likely to make in your calculations (such as forgetting to take a square root or to raise a number to a power). A common trick is to try to mislead you by including these "mistakes" as incorrect answer choices. When you finish the problem, you are excited to see that the answer you calculated was one of the answer choices. In your mind, it must be right, but it's dead wrong! You unknowingly fell into the "likely error trap."

Example 1: If $(x + 5) - (4/2)(6/3) = 12$, what is x?

    a. 3
    b. 7
    c. 9
    d. 11
    e. 13

This is a particularly easy problem; the correct answer is D, or 11. But the other answer choices were not chosen randomly. If you made a mistake at the end and added 1 instead of subtracting 1, you would have gotten an answer of 13, which is answer choice E. If you added the quantity $(4/2)(6/3)$ from $(x + 5)$ instead of subtracting it, you would have gotten 3, which is answer choice A. The other answer choices are other results that you could have gotten if you had made a less likely (but still possible) mistake.

On an easy problem like this, the tactic may not be an issue for you. But, rest assured, the test writers also use the SAME sneaky answer choices on the harder questions. If you get tired and sloppy, they might lure you into a trap. (If the question asks for the x-intercept, you can be fairly certain that the y-intercept will be one of the wrong answer choices!)

Another pitfall is becoming so engrossed in your calculations that you forget what you are being asked.

<u>Example 2</u>; If $(x + 5) - (4/2)(6/3) = 12$, what is $3x$?

     a.   8
     b.   11
     c.   13
     d.   22
     e.   33

At first blush, this problem appears identical to Example 1. In fact, your first step would be to solve for x, just as you did beforehand. When you do, you might be happy to discover your answer (11) as choice C. Most students, in fact, would simply assume they were finished and move onto the next question. The trap they fell into was failing to *verify exactly what the question asked*, which was the value of **3x**, rather than x.   By doing so, they would lose a point on a relatively easy problem that they should have gotten right.

Before you choose your answer, ALWAYS re-read the question stem to make sure that you have calculated the right quantity. Remember: the most common mistakes will always be included as incorrect answer choices. Don't lose points for carelessness!

Strategy 6. Now, let's get down to some actual quantitative traps and pitfalls. According to mathematical rules, when both sides of an inequality are multiplied or divided by a negative number, the inequality is reversed:

<u>Example</u>: If x > y and c < 0, then cx < cy

If we plug in simple numbers for x, y and c (such as 4, 3 and -2, respectively), the concept is easy to understand:

4 > 3 and –2 < 0   Hence, (-2) (4) < (-2)(3) or -8 < -6

Unfortunately, this concept is rarely tested on its own, but in the context of a more difficult problem. A typical "trap" that students fall into is failing to reverse the inequality sign. Be aware of this pitfall for this type of problem. As we've already warned, the wrong answer that you get when you make this mistake will likely be one of the five answer choices.

Strategy 7. Another source of confusion (and a great trap for test writers) is a problem that asks students to calculate the *overall* % increase or % decrease of a price, rate or speed that has changed more than once.   In the final calculation for such problems, the correct denominator is the ORIGINAL whole, not the intermediate one. And, of course, the wrong answers you would get if you used the incorrect denominator will likely be included as answer choices.

<u>Example</u>: A software company discounts its old version of web design software to 50% of its original price. Two months later, when the software has still not sold, the company lists it on eBay at a price that has been reduced by an additional 20%. By what overall percentage has the price been reduced?

     a.   55%
     b.   60%
     c.   70%
     d.   75%
     e.   80%

The most common mistake for this question is to simply add the two % and assume that you have the answer (50% + 20% = 70%). Wrong!

Simply plugging in a few easy numbers will show us the error.   Assume that the software originally cost $100. The first 50% discount reduces its price to $50. The second discount is 20% of $50, or $10, which reduces the price to $40. To calculate the *overall percentage* that the software has been reduced, we must use the original denominator of $100: $60 / $100 = 60%.

Strategy 8. In Strategy 7, we demonstrated the correct way to calculate multiple reductions in percentages. But what if the percentage moves up, then down (or vice versa)? Beware of problems that involve multiple changes in percentages, particularly when they change in opposite directions. The GRE writers love this type for question, which is ripe with potential traps.

Example: Susan purchased a new condo when she moved to Los Angeles. Two years later, after a devastating correction in the housing market, she sold it to her neighbor Nathan for 40% less than she originally paid for it. Nathan did a few quick fixes and re-sold the condo to Janice for 20% more than he paid Susan for it. The price that Janice paid for the condo was what percentage of the original price that Susan paid?

        a.   28%
        b.   40%
        c.   65%
        d.   72%
        e.   80%

The "trap" that many students fall into is simply subtracting 40% and adding back 20%, which leaves an overall loss of 20%. Accordingly, they choose answer choice E.

This answer is wrong, for the same reasons we discussed in Strategy 7. For questions that deal with multiple changes in percentages, the denominators are different for each step. Why? The first change is a reduction of the original price; the second change is an increase of a smaller amount.

Here is the correct approach to the problem. Because the problem works with percentages, we will use 100 as the original price. (We are free to use any number, but since percentages are involved, 100 is the least confusing choice.)

If Susan paid $100 for her condo, then she sold it to Nathan for $60, which is 40% less. Nathan sold the condo to Janice for 20% more than what HE paid for it, which was $60. Nathan therefore sold the condo for $60 + (0.2)($60) = $72.

The question asked us to determine what percentage of Susan's original price Janet paid for the condo. In this case, the correct answer is 72/100, or 72%, which is answer choice D.

Strategy 9. One of the easiest ways to intimidate students is with complicated answer choices, particularly for word problems. The student glances at the answers, which look convoluted and scary, and assumes that the problem is well beyond his/her capability. Don't fall for it! In most cases, the answers appear intimidating because they are written in the form of multiple variables.

Example 1: During an annual promotion, a wholesaler can buy one can of air freshener for p dollars. Each additional can costs k dollars less than the first one, or p − k dollars. Which of the following represents the wholesaler's cost, in dollars, for m cans of air freshener bought during this promotion?

        a. $p + (m − 1)(p − k)$
        b. $p + m(p − k)$
        c. $m(p − k)$
        d. $\{p + (p − k)\} / m$
        e. $(p − k) + (p − k)/m$

You do NOT have to set up simultaneous equations to solve the problem. You don't even have to do many calculations. Just think about what the question is asking. Then, plug in a few numbers and see what you get. Most of the time, these questions are FAR easier than they look.

We want to find the total cost of a certain number of cans of air freshener. Let's randomly let p = 10 and k = 2. This makes p − k = 8. If m = 5, then the cost for the cans would be p + (4)(8). This corresponds to answer choice A, which simply states the same thing using the original variables: $p + (m − 1)(p − k)$.
If this seems confusing, run through the problem a few times with a fresh perspective. Don't be overwhelmed by the multiple variables OR the odd-looking answers. Just think through the question and plug in values. It works.

<u>Example 2</u>: If $(b - 4)^2 = 81$, what is b?

    a.   3
    b.   5
    c.   9
    d.   13
    e.   27

At first glance, you may be tempted to factor out this expression and solve for b. Before you do, stop and consider if there is a faster approach. The equation is essentially asking you to find the number that will make $(b - 4) = 9$, which is the square root of 81. By quickly solving this simpler equation (or just plugging in the answer choices), we can find the correct answer (13) significantly faster than solving the original equation.

<u>Example 3</u>: The Q members of the senior class agree to split the cleanup costs equally for their graduation dance, which will be P dollars. If R students fail to graduate and do not pay their share, but the cleanup costs remain the same, how many additional dollars will each of the remaining students have to contribute to pay the cleanup costs?

    a. $P/(Q - R)$
    b. $(P/Q)(R - Q)$
    c. $PQ/(Q - R)$
    d. $PR/Q(Q - R)$
    e. $PQR/Q(Q - R)$

This "killer" problem is an excellent example of a question that would appear at the very end of the quantitative section of the GRE. Sadly, most students would be too intimidated to even attempt it. From our experience, the fastest and easiest way to solve the problem is to substitute numbers for the variables. For the sake of simplicity, let's assume that Q = 100, P = 1000, and R = 20.

Thus, the cost per person is P/ Q = 1000/100 = 10 dollars. If R = 20 students do not pay their share, then the additional cost for the 100 − 20 = 80 remaining students is (20 X 10) = 200. 200/80 = $2.5 dollars.

Now, we can solve the problem by converting this relationship from numbers to letters. The cost per student is P/Q = 10 dollars. If R = 20 students do not pay their share, then the additional cost for the (Q - R) = 80 remaining students is: (P/Q) (R) / (Q − R) = 20 (1000/100) / (100 − 20) = 20 (10) / 80 = $2.50, which is Choice D.

Strategy 10. This "stay calm and plug in numbers" approach is the best strategy for those annoying word problems that ask you to figure out someone's age or weight based on how it **relates** to that of two other people. At first glance, it seems that you need to set up and solve an equation. You don't. Just pick a few numbers and go.

<u>Example</u>: Liam weights twice as much as Kyle, but 30 pounds less than Zack. If Zack weighs 110 pounds more than Kyle, how much does Zack weigh?

    a.   110
    b.   160
    c.   190
    d.   200
    e.   220

The most important thing to note about this problem is that it gives us no actual weights, just the *relationship* among them. Thus, we are free to choose our own numbers. Let's randomly assume that Liam weighs 160. This means that Kyle weighs half of 160, which is 80. Since Zack weighs 110 pounds more than Kyle, then Zack weighs 80 + 110 = 190, which is answer choice C.

<u>Note</u>: you would have gotten the correct answer, regardless of the number that you picked for Liam's weight. In this problem, the test writers have clearly defined the *relationship* between the three weights, which allowed us to use the "plugging in" technique.

With that in mind, you must ALSO be able to solve word problems with ages and weights that give *actual numbers* for the values. In these cases, you cannot simply plug in numbers. Instead, you must write and solve and equation for the unknown variable.

Example: The sum of Adam's age and Eve's age is 54. Six years ago, Adam was 4 years older than Eve. How old is Eve now?

a. 23
b. 25
c. 26
d. 28
e. 29

This problem gives us the sum of the current ages of Adam and Eve. We also know that Adam was 4 years older than Eve six years ago. Our task is to find Eve's current age. Our first step will be to draw a quick chart for the information we are given:

Name	Current Age	Age 6 years ago
Adam		
Eve		

Since the question asks us to determine Eve's current age, we will let that value = x. Once we do, we know that Adam's current age = 54 - x. Six years ago, Adam's age was (54 –x) – 6 and Eve's age was x – 6.

Name	Current Age	Age 6 years ago
Adam	54 - x	(54 – x) – 6
Eve	x	x – 6

Now, we must write our equation to solve for x. Since we are being asked to solve for Eve's age, we will establish our equation using Adam's *data from six years ago*.

From the table, we know that Adam's age 6 years ago = (54 - x) – 6. From the problem, we ALSO know that Adam was 4 years older than Eve 6 years ago, or (x – 6) + 4. Therefore, (54 -x) – 6 = (x – 6) + 4
x =25 = Eve's current age. Choice B is correct.

Now, let's check our work. If Eve is currently 25, then Adam = 54 – 25 = 29. Six years ago, Adam was 29 – 6 = 23 and Eve was 25 – 6 =19. Eve's age six years ago was indeed 4 less than Adam's age.

Strategy 11. The GRE writers are fascinated with right triangles. In fact, most test preparation materials advise students to memorize the side lengths for the most common right triangles, which are the 3-4-5, 5-12-13 and 7-24-25. From our perspective, it's more important to understand what the Pythagorean theorem actually *means*.

Example: Which of the following sets of numbers *cannot* represent the lengths of the sides of a right triangle?

a. 10, 24, 26
b. 3.7, 11.9, 12.5
c. 9, 26, 31
d. 4, 15, 15.5
e. 15, 36, 39

Although this is a geometry question, it adds an additional level of trickery by asking which answer could NOT be correct. This means that four of the answers COULD be right; your job is simply to find the only wrong answer.

How do you do that, if your only "preparation" was memorizing the three sets of side lengths? It would allow you to eliminate answer choice A, which is a multiple of the 5-12-13 triangle, but you really couldn't go much further. Thankfully, there is a better approach.

74

Instead of memorizing sets of numbers, focus on the actual relationship that is defined by the Pythagorean theorem. *The squares of the two shorter sides MUST equal the square of the third side.* For these five answer choices, run through the calculations as quickly as you can. When you do, you will discover that they are all correct answer choices, except for choice C. If we square 9 and 26, and add those numbers together, they do NOT equal the square of 31. Since the question asks us to identify the *one incorrect answer*, we must choose C.

Strategy 12. Since the GRE provides students with the formulas for the areas of geometric figures, it's an absolute given that the writers will probe whether or not students understand the implications of these formulas. Typical questions will ask what happens to the area of a triangle or rectangle, if one side is lengthened and another is shortened. Alternatively, the writers will ask what happens to the circumference of a circle if its diameter doubles. As you might expect, these questions are filled with traps, pitfalls, and misleading answer choices.

Example 1: If the length of a rectangle increases by 27% and its width decreases by 50%, what is the overall effect on the area of the rectangle?

      a.   It increases by 63.5%
      b.   It decreases by 63.5%
      c.   It increases by 37.5%
      d.   It decreases by 37.5%
      e.   It cannot be determined from the information given.

The area of a rectangle is equal to its length times its width. Therefore, the new area will be equal to the new length (which is 1.27 times its old length) times its new width (which is 0.50 times its old width). Multiplying them together, we find that the new area is (1.27)(0.50), or 0.635 times the original area. Thus, answer choice D is correct.

Example 2: If the diameter of a circle increases by 75%, by what percent will the area of the circle increase?

      a.   75%
      b.   112%
      c.   175%
      d.   206%
      e.   212%

The fastest way to solve this problem is to select values for the diameter of the circle and determine the effect on the area. If the diameter is 4, the radius is 2 and the area is 4 times π. Increasing the diameter by 75% to 7, makes the new radius = 3.5, and the new area is 12.25 times π. The percent increase is (12.25 - 4) / 4 = 8.25/4, or 206%. Choice D is correct.

Strategy 13. Only a few geometry problems on the GRE will be so simple that you can solve them by plugging numbers into formulas. Instead, the writers usually include questions that will require you to APPLY that information to real-world situations. To achieve a top score on the quantitative portion of the GRE, you must be able to work through these geometry problems quickly and efficiently.

Example 1. A plumber wishes to cover a bathroom wall with colorful ceramic tiles, which each measure 1/2 inch by 3 inches. If the wall is a rectangle that measures 10 feet by 12 feet, how many ceramic tiles will the plumber need to complete the job?

      a.   1,152
      b.   1,728
      c.   11,520
      d.   17,280
      e.   25,290

The area of the wall is 10 feet x 12 feet, or 120 square feet. The area of one tile is 1/2 inch x 3 inches = 3/2 square inches, or 1.5 square inches.

First, for simplicity, we must convert the units of the tiles from square inches to square feet:
1.5 square inches (1 square foot/ 144 square inches) = 0.0104166 square feet.

Next, we must multiply the total area of the wall by the area of one tile to determine how many tiles we need:
120 square feet (1 tile/0.0104166 square feet) = 11,520 tiles, which is Choice C.

Example 2: If one cubic foot of water equals 7.8 gallon, how long it take for a faucet that flows at a rate of 8 gallons/minute to file a cube that is 14 feet on each side (in hours)?

        a.   0.75 hours
        b.   44.6 hours
        c.   343 hours
        d.   2675 hours
        e.   2744 hours

Here, it is helpful to visualize a faucet filling up a large cubic tank. A cube with a side of 14 feet has a volume of 14 x 14 x 14 = 2,744 cubic feet.

Since 1 cubic foot = 7.8 gallons, 2,744 cubic feet = 21,403 gallons.

If the faucet flows at a rate of 8 gallons per minute, it will take 21,403/8 = 2,675.4 minutes to fill the cube, or 44.6 hours. Answer choice B is correct.

When you encounter one of these "applied" problems, resist the urge to panic. Stop, read it through and decide whether you have the time to attack it. If you become confused or nervous, skip it until the end of the section when/if you have extra time. Then, apply a logical plan of attack:

1. First, figure out which geometric figure is being discussed. In Example 1, it was a rectangular wall; in Example 2, it was a cubic tank.

2. Determine what measurement of that figure you need to calculate to solve the problem. For two-dimensional objects, it will be likely be area; for three-dimensional ones, it will probably be volume.

3. Use that information to solve the specific problem. With rare exceptions, this will be the easiest step. (According to our students, the hardest part is sifting through all of the initial information and data that are provided to find the actual question that is being asked. Remember: the GRE writers intentionally use a lot of smoke and mirrors to intimidate you. Don't let it happen.)

Strategy 14. From many students' perspective, the worst word problems on the GRE are the "both or neither" type, which ask you to find the percentage (or number of) participants who belong to overlapping groups. Once again, these problems are not nearly as intimidating as they look. In fact, many can be easily reduced to one simple formula.

Example: One hundred vacationers on a cruise ship have signed up for the ship's activities. Sixty sign up for ballroom dancing lessons. Thirty-five sign up for aerobics class. Twenty sign up for neither ballroom dancing nor aerobics class. How many have signed up for BOTH ballroom dancing and aerobics class?

        a.   5
        b.   10
        c.   12
        d.   15
        e.   18

In these problems, the premise might be customers at a restaurant choosing soup and salad or high school student studying Spanish or French. Regardless of the scenario, the approach is the same. You simply need to create an equation to identify and quantify each group. The trick is that the total number of people (in this case 100) includes FOUR groups:

Ballroom dancers   Those doing both
Aerobics students   Those doing neither

Their relationship is defined as follows: Group 1 + Group 2 + Neither – Both = 100

Why must we divide them into 4 groups, rather than 3? Because we don't want to count the people who are doing both activities twice. Once we establish this simple equation, we can plug in numbers to solve for the unknown, which in this case is the group defined as Both.

Group 1 + Group 2 + Neither – Both = 100
60 + 35 + 20 – Both = 100
Both = 15, which is answer choice D.

Strategy 15. Beware of questions in which a single "trick" word, such as **not**, **except** or **but**, changes your entire approach to the problem. We have already shown an example of this question type in Strategy 11, which discussed the Pythagorean theorem. Let's look at another typical example.

Example: Which of the following numbers CANNOT be even?

      a.   The sum of two odd numbers
      b.   The sum of an odd number and an even number
      c.   The product of two even numbers
      d.   The product of an odd number and an even number
      e.   The sum of two even numbers

Here, we have an easy problem that is needlessly complicated by the odd wording of the question stem. If a number cannot be even, then it must be odd. Hence, we must find the one answer choice that MUST be odd. By plugging in numbers to test each answer choice, we can quickly determine that choice B, the sum of an odd number and an even number, is the only one that cannot produce an even number. It is therefore the correct answer.

Strategy 16. Most figures on the GRE are drawn to scale. If they are not, the test writers will advise you, As a general rule, if the GRE provides a figure as an illustration, and notes that it is NOT drawn to scale, the figure is usually presented in a misleading manner. The second that you note the "not drawn to scale" disclaimer, **stop relying on the figure for any sort of guidance or insight.**

Why? The GRE writers have been known to draw triangles in which an angle APPEARS to be 90 degrees, but it is not. Alternatively, it may appear that a line bisects a side of the triangle, when it actually doesn't. The only way to approach these problems is to *disregard the figures* and work solely with the numerical information that you are given. The numbers won't mislead you, but the figure probably will.

Strategy 17. To solve GRE geometry problems, be prepared to break complex figures into smaller, simpler ones. Many times, a diagram will show an odd-shaped polygon and ask you to determine an area, side length or perimeter.   Upon closer inspection, this polygon is actually two triangles that share a common side. Or, it is a rectangle and a triangle that share a common side. These problems are usually easily solved using the Pythagorean theorem or another basic geometric formula. This "trick" is the key to solving a number of geometry questions on the exam.

Example: Jenny is making holiday decorations from a large piece of velvet fabric. How many circles, each with a 6-inch radius, can Jenny cut from a rectangular piece of the fabric, which measures 240 inches x 348 inches?

      a.   290
      b.   558
      c.   580
      d.   1160
      e.   2320

In this case, we are cutting a rectangular piece of fabric into smaller, circular pieces. If the circles have a 6-inch radius, then their diameter is 12 inches. For a piece of fabric measuring 240 inches by 348 inches, we can lay 240/12, or 20 circles across the length of the fabric.

Since the width of the fabric is 348 inches, we can make 348/12, or 29 total rows of circles. Therefore, Jenny can make 20 x 29 = 580 total circles. Answer choice C is correct.

Strategy 18. Be ready to draw a diagram to solve word problems. Older versions of the GRE offered sketches for most geometry problems. Increasingly, however, the test writers will present the problem verbally, which requires students to draw their own diagrams of the scenario. In many cases, a diagram is the fastest way to assess a problem, organize information and find the solution.

Example: A rectangle that measures 12 inches by 24 inches is completely inscribed in a circle. If all four corners of the rectangle touch the circumference of the circle, what is the area of the circle?

    a.   144 π
    b.   180 π
    c.   196 π
    d.   576 π
    e.   720 π

In this situation, the diagonal of the rectangle is equal to the diameter of the circle. Because the rectangle can also be viewed as two triangles that share the diagonal as a common side, we can use the Pythagorean theorem to calculate its length.

Accordingly, the square of the diagonal is equal to (12)(12) + (24)(24) = 144 + 576 = 720. This means that the diameter of the circle is the square root of 720, or 26.8; the radius is therefore 13.4. Now, we can calculate the area of the circle, which is (13.4)(13.4)(π), = 180 π. Choice B is correct.

Strategy 19. Be prepared to read data from graphs and charts. Increasingly, the test writers will present data in a tabulated form and ask questions about percent increases and deceases. Handle the questions the same way you would if the data were presented in non-tabulated form.

Example 1:   **Viscosity Measurements for Sugar Syrups**

Percent Solids	Relative Speed of Flow
20%	50% as fast as syrup with 10% solids
30%	50% as fast as syrup with 20% solids
40%	50% as fast as syrup with 30% solids

According to the table above, sugar syrups with 10% solids flows how many times as fast as syrup with 40% solids?

    a. 2
    b. 4
    c. 8
    d. 16
    e. 32

The data indicate that each 10% increase in solids decreases the flow by 50%. Therefore, the syrup with 10% solids would flow 8 times as fast (2 x 2 x 2) as the syrup with 40% solids. Hence, the correct answer choice is C.

Percentage of Contact Lens Wearers (By Age)

	U.S.	U.K.	France	India
Under 10	2	5	1	0
10 – 18	21	30	15	3
19 – 30	38	35	29	19
31 – 50	29	25	40	66
Over 51	10	5	15	12

2a. If the number of contact lens wearers in France 5 million, and they each own exactly three pairs of lenses, how many of the pairs belong to wearers who are 51 or older?

     a.   450,000
     b.   750,000
     c.   1,500,000
     d.   2,250,000
     e.   4,500,000

In this question, students must use the data in the table, which is presented in %, to determine the number of contact lenses owned by a specific population group.

To solve, just think the problem through carefully. If France has a total of 5 million contact lens wearers, then the number who are 51 or older is (5 million)(0.15) = 750,000. If all of these patients own 3 pairs each, then the number of pairs is **2,250,000**. Choice D is correct.

2b. Which of the following best explains the small percentage of teenage contact lens wearers in India, compared to those in the U.S., the U.K, and France?

     a.   They are unsafe for use
     b.   They are unavailable
     c.   They are prohibitively expensive
     d.   They are legally prohibited for minors
     e.   They are not advertised on Indian television

This question requires students to interpret the data in a logical manner. In this case, contact lenses are obviously available, affordable and safe in India, because older patients wear them. Thus, the most logical explanation for the large discrepancy in use is that the law restricts their use to those 18 and over.

Strategy 20. Also be prepared for convoluted "grouping" problems that cannot be solved unless *you* create a table.

Example. A pet shop had an inventory of 150 animals - 105 of the animals were cats and the rest were dogs. If 85 of the animals are female and 80% of the dogs are female, how many of the pets are male cats?

     a.   9
     b.   36
     c.   45
     d.   49
     e.   56

The most important thing to notice about this problem is that the categories are distinct, with no possibility of overlap. Second, you must note that the test writers have given you enough data to solve the problem, but they have presented it in the most convoluted way possible.

The best way to attack this type of problem is to summarize the data you are given in a simple table. Once you do, the answer will either be obvious – or surprisingly easy to calculate.
In this case, we have cats and dogs in a pet shop; some are male, while others are female.

When we put the information into our chart, we get:

	Cats	Dogs	Total
Male	56	9	65
Female	49	36	85
Total	105	45	150

From the table, we can answer the question; the number of male cats is 56. Choice E is correct.

Strategy 21. If you've tried everything else (substitution, back-solving, etc.) and you STILL can't solve a problem, don't sweat it. *Just guess.* Your chances for success are 20% for multiple choices questions, and even higher if you can eliminate a few incorrect answer choices.

When evaluating the possible answers, immediately rule out the ones that are obviously wrong:

- the question asks you to determine a length, and the answer choice is negative.
- the solution is an integer, but the answer choice is a fraction between zero and one.
- the question asks you to calculate the area in which a circle intersects with a square (which is very tiny), and the answer choice is larger than the size of one of the actual figures.

In all of these situations, at least one (or more) answer choices can immediately be ruled out. The more choices you can eliminate, the greater your odds of guessing correctly.

Strategy 22. On any question, if quantities are expressed in different forms (or units), convert them to the same form before you make any additional calculations. In geometry formulas, convert a given measurement (such as an area, perimeter or volume) to the formula that it represents. Many times, the GRE writers will provide data in different forms as a trap. One (or more) of the incorrect answer choices will be answers that you will get if you fail to convert your units properly.

Example: On the blueprint for a football stadium, 1 foot represents 1/3 mile. If the architect makes an error of 1/16 inch in reading the blueprint, what will be the corresponding error in the actual stadium?

    a.   9.17 feet
    b.   36.67 feet
    c.   48.67 feet
    d. 192.17 feet
    e. 586.17 feet

This is a classic example of an easy problem that is presented in multiple units. To make the units consistent, we can use a simple proportion: 1 foot / 1/3 mile = 1/16 inch / x

Noting that the answer choices are presented in terms of feet, we will convert all of our numbers to feet and solve for x. Since 1 mile = 5,280 feet, our equation is:

1 foot / 1760 feet = 1/192 feet/ x. Thus, x = 1760/192 = 9.17 feet, or answer choice A.

Strategy 23. Be prepared to differentiate between word problems with *simple averages* and those with *weighted averages*. The examples below will illustrate how similar the two problems can look, along with typical pitfalls the GRE writers include.

Example 1: In a kennel with 28 dogs, of which half are neutered and half are intact, the average (mean) weight of the neutered dogs was 83 pounds. If the average weight of the 14 intact dogs in the kennel was 92 pounds, what was the average weight of the entire kennel?

    a. 86.5
    b. 87.0
    c. 87.5
    d. 88.0
    e. 88.5

In this case, the number of intact dogs (14) is equal to the number of neutered dogs (also 14), which means that we can simply take the average of 83 + 92 and apply it to the entire kennel. The result is 87.5, or choice C, which is the correct answer.

The next problem, though, shows what happens when the two groups under consideration are NOT the same size. The calculation becomes more difficult.

Example 2: In a kennel with 27 dogs, the average (mean) weight of the neutered dogs was 83 pounds. If the average weight of the 15 intact dogs in the kennel was 92 pounds, what was the average weight of the entire kennel?

    a.   86.5
    b.   87.0
    c.   87.5
    d.   88.0
    e.   88.5

In this case, the number of neutered and intact dogs in the kennel is not the same, which means that we must take a *weighted average* for each of the two groups.

Here's how to approach a problem with weighted averages:

Total kennel average = (Sum of intact weights + Sum of neutered weights) / Total # of dogs
Now, we must weigh the averages properly in the equation:
Total kennel average = {(15)(92) + (12)(83)} / 27 = 88. The correct answer choice is D.

Strategy 24. The GRE test writers love to ask questions about two or more ratios that represent different quantities. To find the correct answer, students must re-state each ratio so that each one has the same whole. Only then can they be compared properly.

Example 1: Jenny colored several cartons of Easter eggs for her younger sister's kindergarten class. Her final basket included blue, green and pink eggs. If the ratio of the number of blue eggs to green eggs is 8:3, and the ratio of the number of green eggs to pink eggs is 1:2, what is the ratio of the number of blue eggs to pink eggs?

    a.   1:2
    b.   2:1
    c.   3:2
    d.   8:1
    e.   8:6

To find the ratio of blue eggs to pink eggs, we must re-state both ratios so that the number of green eggs is the same in both.

Blue eggs to green eggs = 8:3
Green eggs to pink eggs = 1:2

In this case, the numbers corresponding to green eggs are 3 and 1, respectively. The easiest way to re-state the ratios is to use their least common multiple of 3 and 1, which is 3.

Blue eggs to green eggs = 8:3
Green eggs to pink eggs = 3:6 (which is the same as 1:2)

The ratios are now stated in a form in which the same number (3) refers to green eggs. The ratio of blue to green to pink eggs is 8:3:6. The ratio of blue eggs to pink eggs is 8:6, which is answer choice E.

Example 2. A pet shop received several dozen kittens to sell during the week before Christmas. The group included a colorful selection of Persian, Siamese and Bengal kittens. The ratio of Siamese kittens to Persian kittens is 12:6 and the ratio of Persian kittens to Bengal kittens is 2:14. Assuming 24 of the kittens are Siamese, how many are Bengal?

    a. 28
    b. 36
    c. 72
    d. 84
    e. 168

This problem is loaded with tricks and traps. It is long and confusing; it has multiple ratios that must be re-stated. Even worse, if you encounter it at a point when you are tired and confused, you might not even see what it is you are being asked to calculate.

Relax. Take it one step at a time. To solve this problem, we must first determine the ratio of Siamese to Bengal kittens by stating both original ratios so that the number of Persians is the same in both:

Siamese to Persian 12:6 or 2: 1
Persian to Bengal 2:14 or 1: 7

The ratios are now stated so that the same number (1) refers to Persian kittens. The ratio of Siamese to Persian to Bengal kittens is 2:1:7. Hence, the ratio of Siamese to Bengal kittens is 2:7. We can use this ratio to set up a proportion to determine the number of Bengal kittens in the pet shop: $2/24 = 7/x$. Thus, X = the number of Bengal kittens = 84. Answer choice D is correct.

Strategy 25. For the GRE writers, a popular ploy is to derive a needlessly complicated question for relatively easy topics. Accordingly, look out for convoluted problems with remainders. For most students, the concept of a remainder is fairly simple; it is the number "left over" when a quantity is divided by another number that doesn't go into it evenly. The writers will likely test your knowledge of remainders by a question like this:

Example: What is the least positive integer that is divisible by both 3 and 4 and leaves a remainder of 1 when divided by 5?

    a. 16
    b. 24
    c. 36
    d. 46
    e. 96

There are actually several traps in this seemingly easy question. First, the words *least positive integer* seem to imply that the answer will be the smallest of the answer choices, which is rarely the case. Likewise, if the question asks you to find the greatest or maximum value of something, the correct answer will rarely be the largest answer choice presented. It is simply a ploy that the test writers use to try to tempt the students who are guessing.

The second trap is the inclusion of an answer choice that meets some of the requirements of the question, but not all of them. Choices A and D are not divisible by 3, but they *do* have a remainder of 1 when it is divided by 5. Choice E is a popular choice, because it DOES meet all of the requirements, but it is not the *least* positive integer that does so.

Our advice for questions like this is to attack the two conditions separately. First, eliminate answer choices that are not evenly divisible by 3 and 4. They are obviously wrong, because they violate the first condition in the problem. Then, starting with the *smallest* answer choices (because the question asks for the *least* positive integer), test the remaining answer choices until you find one that fits. Stop there; the first one that fits is the correct answer. In this case, the correct answer is C, or 36.

Strategy 26. Another way the GRE writers complicate seemingly "easy" questions is by changing a single word, which totally changes what you are being asked. If you are in a hurry when you reach the question, or simply misread it, you will likely get the wrong answer. Even worse, you will *think* you got it right, because the answer you calculated shows up as one of the five answer choices. Note the two examples below.

Example 1: What positive integer is 40% less than 15,600?

    a.   4,680
    b.   6,240
    c.   6,864
    d.   8,680
    e.   9,360

Example 2: What positive integer is 40% of 15,600?

    a.   4,680
    b.   6,240
    c.   6,864
    d.   8,680
    e.   9,360

If you glanced quickly at these questions and didn't see the difference, then you fell into the trap. In Example 1, you must find the number that is 60% **of** 15,600, which is *40% less*. The correct answer choice is E, or 9,360. Example 2, however, is asking you to find 40% of 15,600, which is 6,240, or choice B.

On a mathematical basis, these questions are no-brainers. The trick is to read them carefully, to catch which calculation you must make. Under serious stress, even good students can fall into the trap.

Strategy 27. For some questions, the writers will offer an answer choice that reads: "it cannot be determined from the information given." Although many students select this answer for tough questions (which *they* cannot solve), it is usually a trap. In rare situations, however, it IS the correct answer. Consider the following examples.

Example 1: When American Idol auditions were held in New York City, the judges allowed an equal number of men and women to take the stage. At the end of a grueling day, the ratio of female to male singers who advanced to the next round was 3 to 2. At the very end of the day, the judges had a change of heart and agreed to add one additional female singer and one additional male singer to the group that advanced. What is the new ratio of female to male singers?

    a.   3:2
    b.   4:3
    c.   5:4
    d.   6:5
    e.   It cannot be determined from the information given.

Example 2: When American Idol auditions were held in New York City, the judges allowed an equal number of men and women to take the stage. At the end of a grueling day, the ratio of female to male singers who advanced to the next round was 3 to 2. At the very end of the day, the judges had a change of heart and agreed to add one additional female singer and one additional male singer to the group that advanced. If the total number of singers who advanced was 32, what was the original number of men chosen to advance?

    a.   8
    b.   10
    c.   12
    d.   18
    e.   20

Although you can multiply and divide ratios (or parts of them), you cannot simply add or subtract from them, UNLESS you know something about the quantities that they represent. In Example 1, the GRE writers do not tell us anything about the original number of singers (male or female) or how many of them advanced to the next round. We simply have a ratio. Hence, the correct answer is E, we cannot determine the final ratio without additional information.

Example 2 is a different story, because we have been given enough information to solve the problem. In the original scenario, the 3:2 ratio of female to male singers applied to a population of 32 – 2, or 30. Hence, the original 30 selected to advance included 18 women and 12 men (a 3:2 ratio). The correct answer for the original number of men chosen to advance is C, 12.

Strategy 28. Unless a question specifically states that a number is an integer, don't assume that it is. Many times, you must solve problems by substituting numbers for variables to see what "fits." Unless you are specifically told that the variable is a positive integer, always check a positive number, a negative number and a fraction in the equation(s) to see what happens. Note the difference between the following two examples, in which a seemingly insignificant difference in wording makes all the difference in the world.

Example 1: For all k not equal to zero, which of the following are true?

I. $k^2 > k$
II, $13k > 3k$
III. $k + 9 > k$

     a.   I only
     b.   II only
     c.   III only
     d.   I and II only
     e.   I, II and III

Example 2: For all positive integers, which of the following are true?

I. $k^2 > k$
II, $13k > 3k$
III. $k + 9 > k$

     a.   I only
     b.   II only
     c.   III only
     d.   I, and II only
     e.   I, II and III

At first glance, these two examples seem identical; in actuality, they are quite different. For Example 1, we are asked to determine which of the statements are true for all k not equal to zero, which INCLUDES negative numbers and fractions. If we simply plug in positive numbers in place of k, we would conclude that all three statements were correct. However, if we substitute values such as ½ and –6 in place of k, we quickly discover that the only statement that is true for positive numbers, negative numbers and fractions is III. Hence, C is the correct answer choice.

In contrast, Example 2 only requires students to test positive integers in each equation. When we do, we discover that all three of the statements are correct. In this case, the correct answer choice is E.

Strategy 29. Beware of relatively easy word problems that are presented in such a convoluted manner that it is hard to figure out what you are being asked. Before tackling such a problem, make VERY sure that you understand:

     a.   what you are being asked to calculate
     b.   the units in which the answer must be presented

Both are common traps on the GRE, as demonstrated by the following example.

Example: Cement truck 1 can pour 600 gallons of concrete mix in 2.1 hours. Cement truck 2 can pour the same amount in 2.9 hours. How many minutes longer than cement truck 1 would it take cement truck 2 to pour 130,000 quarts of concrete mix?

     a.   48
     b.   126
     c.   432
     d. 2600
     e. 6825

Although the original information is given in hours and gallons, the answer choices are presented in terms of minutes and quarts. This means that the student must make both conversions correctly to get the right answer. We recommend that you complete the conversions first:

Truck 1   2.1 hours/600 gallons = 126 min/600 gallons = 126 min / 2400 qt
Truck 2   2.9 hours/600 gallons = 174 min/600 gallons = 174 min / 2400 qt

Once the data for both cement trucks are converted to the correct units, we can calculate the answer. At this point, it is helpful to look back at the question stem and see exactly what you are being asked. In this case, it is the *difference in times* that the trucks would take to pour 130,000 quarts of concrete. To solve, we must determine the time required by each truck and compare the numbers.

Truck 1   126 min / 2400 qt = 6825 min / 130,000 qt
Truck 2   174 min / 2400 qt = 9425 min / 130,000 qt

9425 − 6825 = 2600, which is answer choice D.

Strategy 30. Be prepared to handle an *average rate* question, which tends to confuse many students. As a result, it is a perennial favorite of the GRE writers. Although it may be presented in a creative way, the format is remarkably similar from test to test:

Two cars, trains or boats will travel from Point A to Point B at different rates of speed.
Two factory workers will assemble widgets at different rates.
Two pumps will deliver water to a tank at different rates.

Whatever the scenario, the student is asked to determine the average rate (or speed) of the activity.

Example: On Valentine's Day, a busy florist drove his delivery truck from Palm Beach to Miami at an average rate of 45 miles per hour. On his return trip to Palm Beach, he encountered rush hour traffic, which slowed him to an average speed of 25 miles per hour. What was the driver's average speed for the trip, in miles per hour?

     a.   30
     b.   32
     c.   35
     d.   36
     e.   38

As you probably suspect, the seemingly obvious answer of 35 mph, which is choice C, is incorrect. When cars travel at different speeds, they take different lengths of time to cover the same distance. Consequently, you cannot simply average the two speeds to get the correct answer. Instead, you must use the following formula to determine the average rate:

Average Rate = Total Distance / Total Time

In this case, the test writers did not give us any specific numbers, so we are free to pick any value for the total distance. In this case, we will use 100 miles for the total distance, which makes each leg of the trip (the distance from Palm Beach to Miami) equal to one-half of 100, or 50 miles.

For the trip from Palm Beach to Miami,
Average Rate = 50 miles/ 45 miles per hour = 1.11 hours

For the return trip from Miami to Palm Beach,
Average rate = 50 miles / 25 miles per hour = 2 hours

Hence, the total time was 3.11 hours

Going back to the original equation, for the total trip,

Average Rate = Total Distance / Total Time = 100 miles/3.11 hours = 32 miles per hour

The correct answer choice is B.

Strategy 31. Another popular question requires students to determine the number of items in a consecutive set, when simply the endpoints are given. The scenario might be:

The number of raffle tickets on a roll.
The number of checks in a check book.
The volumes of encyclopedia on a shelf at the library.

Whatever the scenario, the student must determine the total number of items in a consecutive series. The trick is to determine whether the set is inclusive or exclusive of the endpoints.

Example 1. When an accountant requested her client's sales records for tax season, she received a stack of invoices numbered 00236 through 00435. How many invoices were in the stack?

      a.   198
      b.   200
      c.   201
      d.   300
      e.   301

To count the number of consecutive integers in a set, subtract the endpoints and add 1. In this case, 00435 - 00236 + 1 = 200. The correct answer is B. Sometimes, though, the writers like to spice up the scenario to try to confuse the reader. Here's a potential twist that you might see on the GRE.

Example 2: When an accountant requested her client's sales records for tax season, she received a stack of invoices numbered 00236 through 00435. Upon further examination, however, the accountant realized that invoice numbers 00236 and 00237 were for transactions in the previous tax year, and should not be included in the current year's calculations. How many invoices did the bookkeeper use for this year's calculations?

      a.   197
      b.   198
      c.   199
      d.   200
      e.   201

For this question, you can do the same calculation you did in the previous example and simply subtract 2 from your total. The answer would be 00435 –00236 + 1 = 200 – 2 = 198.

Alternatively, you can do a single calculation, using 00238 as your new endpoint. The result will be the same. 00435-00238+1 = 198. The correct answer is B.

Strategy 32. Be ready for probability problems that try to confuse you with extraneous information. To test a student's knowledge of probability, most textbooks use examples in which someone flips a coin or rolls a pair of dice. In the case of a coin, the probability of a heads is ½, regardless of the number of times the coin is flipped. Likewise, when a single die is rolled, the probability of rolling a 1 is equal to that of rolling any of the other numbers on the die, which is 1/6.

Sometimes, the GRE writers ask questions that are this simple and direct. More often, however, they raise the level of difficulty by presenting a scenario in which multiple events occur, which may (or may not) impact the subsequent ones. Your job is to decide which information is relevant to the question that is being asked, and which is simply a distraction.

Example: At the company picnic, each of the firm's 20 employees placed a raffle ticket into a bowl. At the end of the night, the company president picked one ticket randomly from the bowl and awarded the first prize to Greg. He then picked another ticket randomly from the bowl and awarded the second prize to Pete. Finally, after awarding two more prizes in the same manner, the president picked a fifth random ticket from the bowl and awarded the fifth prize to Jim. Assuming that the first four tickets were not placed back into the bowl after the first four prizes were awarded, what was the probability of Jim winning the fifth prize?

    a.   1.25%
    b.   2.50%
    c.   5.00%
    d.   5.25%
    e.   6.25%

This question is embarrassingly easy to answer. The challenge is to cut through the non-essential details and get to the relevant facts. None of the information about Greg, Pete and the first four drawings relates to Jim's drawing, EXCEPT that the first four winning tickets were removed from the bowl (and not replaced) before drawing number five. Hence, Jim's ticket was one of 16 tickets left in the bowl during the fifth drawing. His probability of winning the prize was 1/16, or 0.0625, which is 6.25%. The correct answer is E.

Strategy 33. The GRE now includes question about geometric probability. In all cases, simply use your knowledge of the shape or figure in question to determine the correct answer.

Example: Marcia places a small circular rock in the center of her circular garden plot. If the plot has a diameter of 84 and the rock has a diameter of 20, what is the probability that any point chosen at random from the garden plot will be beneath the rock?

    a.   5.66%
    b.   11.32%
    c.   20.00%
    d.   23.81%
    e.   25.00%

This question is asking us to find the common area in two concentric circles. The area of the garden plot (the larger circle) is $(42)(42) \pi$, or 1764π, while the area of the rock (the smaller circle) is $(10)(10) \pi$, or 100π. To determine the probability of any given point being in both circles, we simply divide the two quantities and convert to a percentage:

Area of the rock (small circle) / Area of the garden plot (large circle) = $100 \pi / 1764 \pi$, or 0.0566, or 5.66%. The correct answer is choice A.

Strategy 34. In recent years, the GRE has become notorious for including tricky questions regarding series or sequences of numbers. The basic premise is quite simple; a number series is a progression of numbers that are arranged according to a specific design. The easiest ones are arithmetic progressions, such as 3, 5, 7, 9,..... in which each number is two digits greater than the previous one in the series. Likewise, series can include examples such as 2, 4, 16, 256, ..., in which the each number is the perfect square of the preceding number.

If you encounter a series question in the first part of an GRE math section, it will probably be fairly straightforward. If the problem is at the end of the section, though, it will undoubtedly include an added level of difficulty. Here's a common trick:

<u>Example</u>: What is the next term in the following series: 11, 12, 13, 24, 15, 48.......

      a.   14
      b.   17
      c.   36
      d.   96
      e.   None of the above.

If you look carefully, you will see that this example is actually a combination of TWO sub-series. The odd numbers (11, 13, 15 ....) form an arithmetic series, while the even numbers (12, 24, 48, ...) form an arithmetic sequence. The next number in the series will be part of the arithmetic sequence. According to the design, it is 15 + 2, or 17. Choice B is correct.

Strategy 35. Although function problems are usually quite easy on the GRE, many students are needlessly intimidated by the odd notation that the test writers use.   Don't be surprised to see all sorts of unusual keyboard symbols in the formulas, such as

X # Y   a * b   m ^ n   a*b*c*d

The strange symbol just means there is a relationship between the two variables. Your job is to clarify that relationship and to solve the actual equation. To do so, all you need to do is plug numbers and see what happens.

<u>Example</u>: The operation @ is defined for all non-zero p and s by the equation p @ s = p/s. If so, then the expression (p @ s) @ r is equal to:

      a.   p/sr
      b.   s/pr
      c.   psr
      d.   pr/s
      e.   r/ps

This problem, which seems intimidating, is actually very easy to solve. By definition, the symbol @ indicates that we should divide the first number by the second. Therefore, all we need to do is divide the quantity p/s by r.   (p @ s) @ r = (p/s) / r = (p/s)(1/r) = p/sr.   Choice A is correct.

Strategy 36. Be prepared to interpret the graphs of different types of linear and quadratic equations. The GRE writers will test these concepts in several ways. Sometimes, they will show you a graph of a line and ask which one of the answer choices could (or could not) be a point on that line. All you will need to do is use the formula for the slope of the line to find your answer.

Other times, the test writers will ask you to determine the x or y intercept of a line simply from a set of points. These questions are rarely too difficult, but they often include traps:

If the writers ask for you to determine the x-intercept of a line, they will undoubtedly include the y-intercept as one of the answer choices. Likewise, if the calculation is a simple subtraction, don't be surprised if the writers include negative numbers in the calculations, to try to confuse you about the way the line should be drawn. It's a silly mistake, but if you are feeling pressed for time, you may fall into the trap.

<u>Example 1</u>: A line with the equation y = 15x − 30 crosses the x-axis at the point with the coordinates m, n. What is the value of n?

      a.   -30
      b.   -2
      c.   0
      d.   2
      e.   15

The test writers have complicated the problem by asking the student to find a coordinate of a single point (m, n) on the line. Upon further inspection, though, they are simply asking us to find the y-intercept, which is where the line crosses the x-axis. To do so, we simply need to solve the equation for x, when y equals 0. The correct answer is 2, or D. (To no one's surprise, the incorrect answer choices are all numbers you might have calculated if you have misinterpreted the question.

Example 2: In the xy-plane, a circle is centered at the origin and passes through the point (-12,0). What is the area of the circle?

    a. $12/\pi$
    b. 6π
    c. 12π
    d. 24π
    e. 144π

A circle that is centered at the origin and passes through point (-12, 0) has a radius of 12. Therefore, its area is 144π, which is answer choice E.

Example 3: When Parallelogram P is plotted on a graph, it has four endpoints. If three of those points are (3, 1), (-1, -3) and (-3, 0), what is the fourth endpoint?

    a.   (-4, 1)
    b.   (-1, 4)
    c.   (4, 1)
    d.   (0, -3)
    e.   (1, 4)

Choice E is correct. To solve, you should plot the first three points, which will give you an idea of what the parallelogram looks like. It will ALSO allow you to eliminate answer choices that are in the wrong quadrant, such as Choices A, B, and D. Once you narrow down to Choices C and E, you can confirm the correct choice by their slopes.

Strategy 37. Although they are less common on the new GRE, work problems may still appear on the exam. They take several forms:

Two girls making a dress
Two boys mowing a lawn
Two workers painting a shed

Whatever the premise, the underlying scenario will involve two people doing the same job at the same time, but at *different rates*. Your job is to use the basic rate equation to solve for the unknown quantity: Rate x Time = the amount of work completed.

Example 1: Gina and Hillary have a small web design business. Gina can design a web site for Client A in 2 hours. Hillary can design the same site in 3 hours. How long will it take them in minutes to design the site if they both work at the same time?

    a.   60
    b.   66
    c.   72
    d.   90
    e.   100

In this case, you must solve the equation for the total time (T) that is needed to complete the job. First, figure the amount of work that each girl does as a percentage of the total amount:

Gina   Rate x Time = Work   (1/2) times T = ½ T
Hillary Rate x Time = Work   (1/3) times T = 1/3T

Now, we must add them together to figure the total time for the job:

½ T + 1/3 T = 1 or 3/6T + 2/6T = 1 or 3T + 2T = 6

Solving for T, we find that Gina and Hillary can complete the job in 1.2 hours if they work together, or 72 minutes. Answer choice C is correct.

Example 2: Gina can design a web site for Client B in 8 hours. Hillary can design the same site in 12 hours. If Hillary arrives two hours late to help Gina with the site, how long will it take both of them to design the web site on that day?

     a.   2.8
     b.   3.6
     c.   5.6
     d.   6.5
     e.   8.0

In this case, we attack the problem the same way as in Example 1, but we must make a small adjustment in the formula to account for the additional work done by Gina:

Gina   Rate x Time = Work   (1/8) times T = 1/8 T
Hillary Rate x Time = Work   (1/12) times T = 1/12T

Since Hillary started two hours late, Gina had already completed (2)(1/8), or 2/8 of the work by the time Hillary arrived.. Hence, our new equation is: 2/8 + 1/8 T + 1/12T = 1

Solving the problem (using 24 as the least common denominator), we find that Gina and Hillary can complete the job together in 3.6 hours. Most students, unfortunately, would fall into the trap of selecting this as the correct answer choice, but it is not.   Look back at what the question asks; then look at what we just calculated. They are NOT the same thing.

The 3.6 hours is the amount of time that Gina and Hillary worked *together* on the web site. Since Gina had already worked for 2 hours before Hillary arrived, the *total time to complete the site that day* (which is what the question asks) is 2 + 3.6 = 5.6 hours, or answer choice D.

If the answer is confusing to you, re-read both examples until you thoroughly understand the difference between the two problems. Example 2 is tricky. It's easy to miss. And it's a classic trap on the GRE.

Strategy 38. Most algebraic word problems on the GRE require students to find the value of a single unknown (x). Some situations, however, involve two unknowns (x and y) and two separate equations. To solve, students must eliminate the same variable in both equations by addition, subtraction, multiplication, or substitution.

Example 1: The Boston Philharmonic charges $50 for adult tickets to their concerts and $20 for children's tickets. If they sold 800 tickets in a given weekend and received $25,000 in total ticket sales, how many adult tickets were sold?

     a.   300
     b.   400
     c.   500
     d.   600
     e.   700

In this case, we can write two equations – one for the number of tickets and the other for their cost. As always, we must first define our variables. We will let = x the number of adult tickets and y = the number of children's tickets.

90

The first equation, which defines the *number* of tickets sold, is x + y = 800
The second equation, which defines the *cost* of the tickets, is 50x + 20y = 25,000

To solve the problem for x, we must combine the equations in a way that eliminates y. The fastest way is to re-write equation 1 as y = 800 – x and substitute this value for y into equation 2.

When we do, we get
50x + 20(800 – x) = 25,000
50x + 16,000 – 20x = 25,000
30x = 9,000
x = 300 adult tickets sold. Choice A is correct.

Example 2: A clothing shop sells six pairs of shoes and eight pairs of socks for $995. The cost for four pairs of shoes and twelve pairs of socks is $750. How much would it cost to buy one pair of shoes?

     a. $58.12
     b. $69.75
     c. $77.50
     d. $139.50
     e. $148.50

In this case, we can write one equation for the first condition and a second equation for the second condition. As always, we must first define our variables. We will let = x the cost of one pair of shoes and y = the cost of one pair of socks.

The first equation, which defines the first condition, is 6x + 8y = 995
The second equation, which defines the second condition, is 4x + 12y = 750

To solve the problem for x, we must combine the equations in a way that eliminates y. We can do this by multiplying the first equation by 3 and the second equation by 2. When we do, we get

18x + 24y = 2,985
8ex+ 24y = 1,500

If we subtract the second equation from the first, we get 10x = 1,485. Therefore, x = $148.50 = the cost of one pair of shoes. Choice E is correct.

Strategy 39. Our final strategy is for geometry problems in which the answers are stated as two terms, such as 4 + 2 π. Ideally, you will understand the question well enough to calculate the correct answer. If you cannot solve the problem, however, or if you simply run out of time, here is a helpful guessing strategy:

Look at the first term in all five answers. Jot down what value appears most often. Then look at the second term in all five answers. Write down the value that appears most often. Choose the answer choice that includes BOTH of these terms:

Example: The final answer choices for a (seemingly hopeless) geometry question are:

     a.   3 + 2 π
     b.   6 + 4 π
     c.   3 + 1 π
     d.   3 + 4 π
     e.   12 + 4 π

The most common term in the first half of the answers is 3. The most common term in the second half of the answers is 4 π. Choose the answer choice with both of these terms, which is D, 3 + 4 π. Statistically, this choice has the highest probability of being correct.

Strategy 40. Develop a specific plan to tackle **quantitative comparisons**, which require you to determine which quantity is greater.... or whether you have enough information to reach that conclusion. A few of our tips are strategies are identical to those for multiple choices questions:

a. Know the directions cold, so that you don't even have to look at them on the day of the exam.

Each question has two quantities to be compared: one in Column A and one in Column B. Compare the quantities taking into consideration any other information given and choose

Answer A - if the quantity in Column A is greater
Answer B - if the quantity in Column B is greater
Answer C - if the two quantities are equal
Answer D - if the relationship cannot be determined without further information.

b. Know what you are – and *aren't* – being asked to do. Quantitative comparisons simply require you to identify which quantity is larger.... or whether you can make that determination for the information that is given. You may – or may NOT – have to perform any calculations to compare the quantities. You also may not have to obtain the exact answer to a math problem – you simply need to determine which quantity is larger. From our experience, many students waste a lot of time on the GRE because they fail to make these distinctions. Don't do any more work than you need to.

c. To make a comparison easier, make the two quantities look alike. Consider the problem to be a simple equality: whatever you do to one side (addition, subtraction, multiplication, division), you must do to the other.

Column A	Column B
148/4	(8)(4)(3)

In this case, Column A contains a fraction, while Column B contains a product of three numbers. To determine which quantity is larger, you must convert them both to whole numbers. When you do, you will discover that Column A = 148/4 = 37, while Column B = (8)(4)(3) = 96. Choice A is correct.

d. Whenever possible, cancel out numbers and expressions that are common to both sides. By doing so, you can easily see the comparison that you are being asked to make.

Column A	Column B
{(4)(8)(2)(3)}/6	{(8)(4)(3)(9)}/6

In this case, both columns include (8)(4)(3) in the numerator and 6 in the denominator. If we cancel these numbers, we can quickly see that Column A = 2, while Column B = 9. Choice B is correct.

e. If one of the quantities contains a variable, you will need to plug-in *several* numbers to ensure that the relationship holds for positive numbers, negative numbers, zero, and fractions. For simplicity, test -1, 0, 1, 2 and ½.

Column A	Column B
X^3	X^2

At first blush, it would seem that the cube of a number would be larger than its square. If X = a positive integer greater than 1, this is certainly the case. But, if X = ½, then its cube is 1/8, which is less than its square (¼). The relationship no longer holds. Thus, Choice D is correct.

f. If the relationship between the values in Column A and B varies when you plug-in different variables, then you *MUST choose Choice D*. The relationship between the two quantities cannot be defined with 100% certainty.

g. For problems that contain *two* variables, you must ALSO check the situation in which X = Y to ensure that the same relationship holds.

Column A	Column B
XY^3	YX^3

If X = Y, the two columns are equal. If not, the relationship of the two quantities will depend upon the value you select for X and Y. Choice D is correct.

h. If Columns A and B contain numbers (and not variables), then a definitive relationship can *always* be determined. In these cases, Choice D is *never* correct.

i. Be wary of situations in which the writers mention someone's annual pay - make sure that you distinguish gross earnings from net (after-tax) earnings when you make your calculations.

Example: Rick earns $6,000 per month, but pays 1/3 of his gross income in taxes. He saves 1/7 of his take-home pay each month, but he receives no interest on the money.

Column A	Column B
The dollar amount that Rick saves per year	$10,286

First, we must determine Rick's take-home pay, which is $6,000 (2/3) = $4,000 per month. If he saves 1/7 of it every month for one year, he will save $4,000(1/7)(12) = **$6,857.14**. Column B, however, does not list this amount. Instead, it lists the amount of money that Rick would save if his *take-home* pay was $6,000 per month (which is a common mistake that students make). If you fell into this trap, you would pick Choice C because the columns would appear to be equal. However, since Rick's annual savings are $6,857.14, Choice B is correct.

j. Be prepared for questions that provide a lot of numbers - but omit the most important one. You can waste a lot of time on these comparisons if you don't notice the omission.

Example: Jenny's monthly budget includes $600 for rent, $300 for her car payment, $100 for insurance, $300 for utilities, and $300 for groceries. Her annual salary before taxes is $50,000.

Column A	Column B
The percentage of Jenny's income that is left for discretionary spending	25%

At first glance, it's obvious what you need to do to solve this problem - add the expenses and subtract the total from Jenny's monthly take-home pay. But, wait. Before you take the time to add these numbers, you need to know the amount of Jenny's take-home pay..... which the writers have not given you. Therefore, there's no need to add a single thing - you don't have enough information to compare the columns, which means that Choice D is correct.

Strategy 41. Now that you've learned the strategies, try your hand at some sample problems. The answers are presented at the end of this chapter.

1. Which of the following is equal to 0.0000543?

    a. 54.3×10^7
    b. $54.3c\ 10^{-7}$
    c. 543×10^{-8}
    d. 5.43×10^{-6}
    e. 5.43×10^{-5}

2. (75% x 800) + (1/6 x 600) =

    a.   660
    b.   700
    c.   1060
    d.   1200
    e.   1400

3. The difference between (X + Y) and (X – Y) is 6. Find the smaller of the two numbers if XY is 30.

    a.   2
    b.   3
    c.   5
    d.   6
    e.   10

4. Simplify the following expression: $(x^4y^7/x^5y^6)^4$

    a. y^3x^2
    b. y^4/x^4
    c. $(y/x)^{12}$
    d. y^{28}/x^{20}
    e.   none of the above

5. If 1/32 of the daily dose of a medication is 3g, what is the total weekly dose of the medication?

    a.   32 g
    b.   64 g
    c.   96 g
    d.   336 g
    e.   672 g

6. The average (mean) of eight numbers is 8. If 2 is subtracted from each of four of the numbers, what is the new average?

    a.   5.5
    b.   6
    c.   6.5
    d.   7
    e.   7.5

7. What is 0.005% expressed as a fraction?

    a.   5/100
    b.   5/250
    c.   5/200
    d.   1/250
    e.   1/200

8. Simply $\sqrt{7}$ $\sqrt{8}$ $\sqrt{9}$

    a.   6.90
    b.   18.75
    c.   20.75
    d.   22.05
    e.   22.45

9. If $x = 10$, what is the value of $x^2 + 1/x^2$?

    a.   100.001
    b.   100.01
    c.   101.1
    d.   101.01
    e.   110.01

10. What is the absolute value of twice the difference of the roots of the equation $5y^2 - 20y + 15 = 0$?

    a.   0
    b.   1
    c.   2
    d.   3
    e.   4

11. A chef must blend a gourmet cheese that costs $25 per pound with processed cheese spread that costs $10 per pound to make a 2000-pound batch that costs $20 per pound. How many pounds of the gourmet cheese can the chef use?

    a.   333
    b.   1,000
    c.   1,333
    d.   1,500
    e.   4,000

12. Joe rented a moving truck for $50 per day plus an additional charge for mileage. If Joe kept the truck for five days, traveled 600 miles during that time, and was charged a total of $550 for the rental, what was the charge for each mile?

    a.   25 cents
    b.   30 cents
    c.   50 cents
    d.   75 cents
    e.   85 cents

13. Olivia purchased carpeting for her family room, which measures 12 feet x 24 feet. If the carpet she selected costs $14 per square yard, how much will it cost Olivia to purchase enough of this carpet to cover her entire family room?

    a. $448
    b. $896
    c. $1,344
    d. $2,016
    e. $4,032

14. For the repeating decimal 0.975634975634975634......, what is the 75th digit to the right of the decimal point?

      a. 3
      b. 4
      c. 5
      d. 6
      e. 7

15. If the base of a parallelogram decreases by 25% and the height increases by 90%, by what percent does the area increase?

      a. 37.5%
      b. 42.5%
      c. 55.5%
      d. 65.0%
      e. 75.0%

16. If x + 7 is an even integer, the sum of the next three even integers is:

      a. 3x + 4
      b. 3(x +7)
      c. 3x + 28
      d. 3x + 33
      e. $(x + 7)^3$

17. Which of the following is a multiple of 10, 15 and 35?

      a.   70
      b.   150
      c.   350
      d.   525
      e. 1050

18. What is the sum of the following fractions: 1/15, 2/10, 2/5, 1/3, 3/30

      a. 11/10
      b. 29/30
      c. 14/15
      d. 31/30
      e. 32/30

19. If x ^ y = xy − y + y^2, then 2 ^ 4 =

      a. 4
      b. 16
      c. 20
      d. 24
      e. 68

20. Greg and Jenny measured their rectangular garden plot for a privacy fence. If the ratio of the length to width was 25:60, what was the diagonal of the enclosed area?

    a.   45
    b.   65
    c.   75
    d.   90
    e.   It cannot be determined from the information given.

21. What is the probability of getting a white jelly bean from a dispenser that contains 28 red jelly beans, 48 green ones, 36 purple ones, 26 pink ones, 30 blue ones and 28 white ones?

    a.   1/8
    b.   1/7
    c.   1/6
    d.   1/5
    e.   ¼

22. Heidi bought U wedding favors at a bridal shop at a price of V per favor. Afterwards, Heidi had W dollars left over. Assuming that she made no other purchases, how much money (in dollars) did Heidi bring to the bridal shop for favors?

    a.   UVW
    b.   UV + W
    c.   (U/V) + W
    d.   UV – W
    e.   It cannot be determined from the information given.

23. Pipe A can fill a tank in 40 hours. Pipe B can fill the same tank in 72 hours. Pipe C can empty the tank in 96 hours. If all three pipes are open at the same time, how many hours will it take to fill the tank?

    a.   20
    b.   35
    c.   40
    d.   56
    e.   60

Refer to the chart below for questions 24 & 25.

Number of Cardiac Patients per Thousand Residents

Atlanta	56
Boston	94
Chicago	87
Detroit	79
Los Angeles	99
Miami	48
Sacramento	61

24. Based on the chart, which city has the third highest number of cardiac patients per thousand residents?

    a.   Los Angeles
    b.   Miami
    c.   Chicago
    d.   Detroit
    e.   Atlanta

25. A physician wishes to visit the two cities that have the closest number of cardiac patients as the number in Omaha, which has 68 patients per thousand residents. According to this chart, which two cities should the physician visit?

      a.   Sacramento and Atlanta
      b.   Sacramento and Detroit
      c.   Atlanta and Detroit
      d.   Atlanta and Miami
      e.   Detroit and Chicago

Each question has two quantities to be compared: one in Column A and one in Column B. Compare the quantities taking into consideration any other information given and choose

Answer A - if the quantity in Column A is greater
Answer B - if the quantity in Column B is greater
Answer C - if the two quantities are equal
Answer D - if the relationship cannot be determined without further information.

26. **Column A**   **Column B**

The number of two-digit positive integers   2
that are multiples of both 7 and 9?

27. George earns a base salary of $300 each week, plus a 20% commission on all sales. During the week of July 1, George sold $15,000 in merchandise

Column A   **Column B**

George's total earnings the week of July 1 $3,300

28. Five consecutive odd integers have a sum of 475.

Column A   **Column B**

159   The largest of the five integers

29. For a circle whose center is F, arc GH contains 40 degrees.

Column A   **Column B**

140   The number of degrees in angle GFH

30. Jade placed a large sum of money in a bank CD that pays 8% simple interest per year. Then, she deposited the same amount, plus an additional $5000, in a real estate investment trust (REIT) that paid 12% simple annual interest. Jade's total annual return from both investments is $26,000.

Column A   **Column B**

The amount that Jade places in the bank CD $125,000

98

31. Sam is five times as old as Greg. Lori is 15 years older than Sam. Their combined age is 81.

Column A	Column B
Greg's age	5

32. The ratio of the areas of Circle A and Circle B is 16π to 36π.

Column A	Column B
The ratio of the circumference of Circle A to Circle B	2/3

33. Clare earns $675 per week as an accountant, but she pays 15% of her earnings in taxes.

Column A	Column B
$29,895	Claire's yearly take home pay

34.

Column A	Column B
The average of five consecutive even integers whose sum is 850	170

35, Jill's boyfriend asked her to bring four DVDs from her collection of eight to a weekend party.

Column A	Column B
1680	The number of different combinations

Answer Key for Quantitative Problems

1. 5.43×10^{-5}. Choice E is correct.

2. (3/4 x 800) + (1/6 x 600) = 600 + 100 = 700. Choice B is correct.

3. The easiest way to solve this problem is to try each answer choice. We know that the product of X and Y is 30; the problem asks us to identify the *smaller* of the two numbers. Therefore, we will substitute each answer choice into the formula $(X + Y) - (X - Y) = 6$ to see which combination gives us the correct an answer. When we do, we discover that (10 + 3) – (10 – 3) = 6. Additionally, (10)(3) = 30. The correct answer is 3, or choice B.

4. $(x^4y^7/x^5y^6)^4 = (y/x)^4 = y^4/x^4$. Choice B is correct.

99

5. We can solve this problem using a simple proportion. First, we must determine the daily dose. 0.03125 / 3g = 1.00 / X, so X = 96 g = the daily dose of the medication. The weekly does is 96 x 7 = 672 g. Choice E is correct.

6. Choice D is correct. If 8 numbers have an average of 8, their sum is 64. Subtracting 2 from 4 of the numbers removes 2(4), or 8 from the sum. The new sum is 56 and the new mean is 56/8 =7.

7. 0.005% = 0.5/100 = 5/1000 = 1/200. Choice E is correct.

8. (2.646)(2.828)(3) = 22.45. Choice E is correct.

9. If x = 10, then $x^2 + 1/x^2$ = 100.+ 0.01 = 100.01. Choice B is correct.

10. Choice E is correct. First, factor the 5 out of the original equation and then divide each side by five. The trinomial factors into (y - 3)(y - 1) = 0. Setting each term to 0 yields y = 3 and y = 1. The difference is 2. Two times two equals 4.

11. First, we must draw a table with the information that we know.

Ingredient	Quantity	Price/pound	Total Cost
Gourmet cheese	x	$25	$25x
Processed cheese	2,000 – x	$10	$10(2,000 – x)
Blend	2,000	$20	$40,000

Since the problem asks us to calculate the amount of gourmet cheese the chef can use, we will let that value = x. Therefore, the amount of processed cheese = 2000 – x. Once we label our variables, we can write the expression for the total cost of each ingredient. From the problem, we can also calculate the cost of the final blend.

Since the cost of the gourmet cheese plus the cost of the processed cheese equals the total cost of the blend, then our equation becomes:

Cost of Gourmet Cheese + Cost of Processed Cheese = Total Cost
25x + 10(2,000 – x) = 40,000
25x + 20,000 – 10x = 40,000
15x = 20,000
x = 1,333 pounds of gourmet cheese. Choice C is correct.

12. The total charge ($550) for the truck was based on the number of days Joe rented it plus the cost per mile. $550 = ($50 per day)(5 days) + (600 miles)(X per mile). If we solve this equation, we find that 600x = 300, so X = 0.50 or 50 cents per mile. Choice C is correct.

13. First, we must convert our room measurements into yards: 12 feet = 4 yards, while 24 feet = 8 yards. Therefore, the area of Olivia's room is (4)(8) = 32 square yards. (32)(14) = $448. Choice A is correct.

14. In this decimal, the repeating pattern is 975634, which is a string of 6 digits. The first 72 digits will be 12 repetitions of this pattern. Then, in the *thirteenth* repetition, the 75th digit to the right of the decimal point will be the *third* number in the series, which is 5. Choice C is correct.

15. The area of the original parallelogram = Base X Height. Let B = the length of the base and H = the height of the original parallelogram.

If the base decreases by 25%, it becomes 0.75B. If the height increases by 90%, it becomes 1.90H. The new area is therefore: (0.75)(1.90) = 1.425, which is 42.5% bigger than the original area. Choice B is correct.

16. $(x + 9) + (x + 11) + (x + 13) = \mathbf{3x + 33}$. Choice D is correct.

17. Choice E, 1050.

18. Convert all fractions to the form with an LCD of 30. The sum is:

$2/30 + 6/30 + 12/30 + 10/30 + 3/30 = 33/30 = 11/10$. Choice A is correct.

19. If $x \wedge y = xy - y + y^2$, then $2 \wedge 4 = (2)(4) - 4 + 16 = 20$. Choice C is correct.

20. This is one of those annoying "trick" questions for which the GMAT is notorious. Most students scramble furiously to calculate an area by using the numbers in the ratio, but it is not necessary. If the ratio of the length to width is 25:60, then the diagonal will be **65,** because it is a multiple of a 5-12-13 special triangle. Choice C is correct.

21. First, we must determine the total number of jelly beans: $28 + 48 + 36 + 26 + 30 + 28 = 196$. Then, we can determine the probability of choosing one of a specific color: $28/196 = \mathbf{1/7}$. Choice B is correct.

22. We can solve this problem by plugging in numbers or by doing a few simple "backwards" calculations. First, let's plug- in numbers.

Let's assume that Heidi bought 10 favors at a price of 2 dollars per favor. Let's also assume that she had 5 dollars left over. Hence, U = 10, V = 2 and W = 5. Heidi therefore spent (10)(2), which is UV. If she had 5 dollars left over, then her original amount of money was **UV + W**. Choice B is correct.

Option 2. If you don't want to plug in numbers, you can just reason the problem through. If Heidi bought U wedding favors, which cost V dollars each, then she spent UV. Finally, she had W cents left over, which we must add to her total amount of money. When we do, we get the same answer as we did with the plug-in method: UV + W.

23. Our unknown is the total amount of time needed to fill the tank, which is the sum of the intake pipes, minus the drain pipe. Hence, our equation is $1/40 + 1/72 - 1/96 = 1/x$. To solve, we must multiply both sides of the equation by 4320x, which is our least common denominator:

$108x + 60x - 45x = 4320$
$123x = 4320$
$x = \mathbf{35.12}$ hours. Choice B is correct.

24. Chicago. Choice C is correct.

25. Sacramento and Detroit. Choice B is correct.

26. The two-digit positive integers that are multiples of 9 are 18, 27, 36, 45, 54, 63, 72, 81, 90, and 99. Of these, only 63 is *also* a multiple of 7. Hence, the correct answer is 1. Choice B is correct.

27. George's total earnings = base salary + commissions = $300 + $15,000(0.20) = $3300. Choice C is correct.

28. Our equation is: $x + (x + 2) + (x + 4) + (x + 6) + (x + 8) = 785$, which simplifies to $5x + 20 = 785$, or $5x = 765$. Therefore, $x = 153$, $X + 2 = 155$, $X + 4 + 157$, $X + 6 = 159$, $x + 8 = 161$. The largest number is 161. Choice B is correct.

29. According to the problem, angle F = 40 degrees. Since it is a central angle, it creates an isosceles triangle within the circle, with GF and FH as equal sides. Angles G and H are therefore equal, with a sum of 180 - 40 = 140 degrees. Angle YXZ is therefore 70 degrees. Choice A is correct.

30. Let x = the amount in the bank CD; x + 5000 = the amount in the REIT
Interest = Principal x Rate x Time. In this case, we know the total amount that Jade earned per year, which is the sum of the two individual investments. So,

$X(0.08)(1) + (x + 5000)(0.12)(1) = 26,000$
$8x + 12(x + 5000) = 2,600,000$
$20x = 2540000$
$x = \$127,000$ in bank CD. Choice A is correct.

31. In this problem, we know the relationship among the ages of Sam, Lori, and Greg – and their combined age. We can use this information to build an equation to solve for Lori's age.
We will let Greg's age = x. Thus, Sam's age is 5x, while Lori's age 5x + 15. Since the sum of their ages is 81, our equation becomes:
$x + 5x + (5x +15) = 81$
$11x + 15 = 81$
$11x = 66$
$x = 6 =$ Greg's age. Choice A is correct.

32. The ratio of the areas of Circle A to Circle B is $16\pi/36\pi$. Since the area of each circle is πr^2 then the radius of Circle A = 4 and the radius of Circle B is 6. We can use this information to calculate the circumference of each.

The circumference of Circle A $=2\pi r = 2\pi(4) = 8\pi$
The circumference of Circle B $=2\pi r = 2\pi(6)= 12\pi$
The ratio of the circumferences of Circle A to Circle B = 8/12 or 2/3. Choice C is correct.

33. Clare's total earnings are $675 (52) = $35,100(0.85) = $29,835.00 Choice A is correct.

34. The average is simply 850/5 = 170. Choice C is correct.

35. Use the factorial formula to solve: $8! / 4! = (8 \times 7 \times 6 \times 5 \times 4 \times 3 \times 2 \times 1) / (4 \times 3 \times 2 \times 1) = 1680$ different combinations. Choice C is correct.

As we end this chapter, we encourage you to re-read the strategies at your leisure. If you need additional practice, we strongly recommend our companion publication, which offers more than 600 sample problems and explanations: *Killer Math Word Problems for Standardized Tests (SAT, GRE, GMAT): When Plugging Numbers into Formulas Just Isn't Enough* (ISBN: 978-1-933819-46-4). Use this book to master the trickiest word problems you are likely to see on the quantitative section of the GRE.

Chapter 8: Final Strategies for Individual Success

After reading the first seven chapters, many students are overwhelmed by the number of strategies and questions that we have presented. Don't jump ship now! Your next step is actually the most critical one: developing a specific plan to master those strategies for the day of the test.

From our experience, no two students have the same strengths or needs; subject areas that are easy for one student can be incredibly difficult for another. To whatever extent possible, you should use this publication to assess your needs. Then, develop a plan to address them.

Strategy 1. For students who desire a comprehensive review of ALL topics that are tested on the GRE, including 1000 realistic practice questions (and solutions), we are proud to offer *Guerrilla Review for the GRE: 1,001 Practice Questions & Answers* (ISBN: 978-1-933819-42-6). Use this publication to boost your skills in the most critical areas and to build your confidence with difficult question types.

For students who need additional practice for the quantitative section of the exam, *Killer Math Word Problems for Standardized Tests (SAT, GRE, GMAT): When Plugging Numbers into Formulas Just Isn't Enough* (ISBN: 978-1-933819-46-4) offers a complete review of the thirty types of word problems you are likely to see, including 600 sample problems. Learn how to answer these questions quickly and accurately on the day of the test.

Finally, for students who are comfortable with the concepts on the GRE and **really** want to challenge themselves before the big day, we are delighted to offer *The Toughest GRE Practice Test We've Ever Seen* (ISBN: 978-1-933819-45-7). Use this publication – and complete the mock exam - AFTER you have completed your preparation program. See how your performance compares to those of other highly competitive students.

These publications are easy to read and affordably priced. Our objective, as always, is to offer the best resources to as many students as possible.

Strategy 2. As you prepare for the test, set realistic (but achievable) goals for your performance. Depending on the amount of time you have to prepare, you might commit to the following:

> learning 20 new words per day
> reviewing 3 math concepts per day

Since no two students are alike, no two study plans will be identical, either. The important thing is to develop (and stick to) a plan that works best for YOU.

Strategy 3. Students with documented learning disabilities (such as ADHD) may qualify for special accommodations for the GRE, including extra time on each section of the exam. The requirements for these accommodations are fairly rigid; if you believe that you may qualify, please review the ETS official requirements at:

http://www.ets.org/portal/site/ets/menuitem.c988ba0e5dd572bada20bc47c3921509/?vgnextoid=ed32486227855010VgnVCM10000022f95190RCRD&vgnextchannel=c9d7be3a864f4010VgnVCM10000022f95190RCRD

Strategy 4. Because of its perceived importance in the graduate school admissions process, the GRE inspires a sense of panic and dread in many students. As a result, many of them, regardless of their intelligence, GPA or study plan, will psyche themselves out on the day of the exam. To whatever extent possible, try to avoid this "all or nothing" mentality.

I know what you're thinking; it is easier said than done. How in the world can you stay calm when so much is at stake? Well, first, it helps to keep the GRE in perspective. Yes, it is an important exam; many programs base their admission decision at least partially on your GRE scores. But here's the FULL context of the test:

It is highly predictable in format and content, which makes it extremely easy to prepare for. By reading this publication, you have acquired considerable insight into the tricks and traps that the writers use, which will give you a competitive edge

Whenever you start to feel overwhelmed, take a step back and put your concerns into the proper context. Then, channel that energy into something constructive, like preparing for the exam!

Strategy 5. After the exam, if you are not satisfied with your scores, don't feel defeated or depressed. Remember, the GRE is, at best, simply ONE piece of information that colleges use in the admissions process. An increasing number of programs no longer require GRE scores; other universities request them, but do not use them to screen or rank applicants. Depending on where you choose to apply (and the strength of your overall application), a disappointing GRE score may not be a deal-breaker.

From our experience, the GRE does not define the intrinsic personal strengths that are essential to succeed, such as integrity, motivation and passion. Over the years, we have seen a number of students who earned top GRE scores fail in other aspects of life, because of deficiencies that were not measured by the exam. Just as often, we have seen students who earned average GRE scores build successful and satisfying careers in fields they were passionate about.

No doubt about it - your GRE score may influence your ability to get into a select group of U.S. colleges and universities. It will **not**, however, define who you are, what you will accomplish, and the contribution you will eventually make to society. By all means, do your best on the test; you should put your best foot forward in the entire application process. But don't fall into the trap of thinking that your score defines you. You are more – *much more* – than the results of a one-day test.

We hope that this publication provides guidance and direction for all aspects of your GRE preparation. To date, we have received overwhelmingly positive feedback from students who have studied the strategies and applied them on the day of the test. We want YOU to enjoy the same benefits, which will help to open the door to the university of your choice.

Use this information for everything it is worth. Seize your destiny!

Appendices

Appendix 1. Learning Words by their Prefixes, Roots & Suffixes

Prefixes and Roots (With Commonly Tested Examples)

A, AN- not, without
amoral, atrophy, asymmetrical, anonymity, anomaly

AB - from, away, apart
abnormal, abdicate, aberration, abhor, abject, abjure, abortive, abrogate, abscond

AC, ACR- sharp, sour
acid, acerbic, acute, acumen, acrid, acrimony

AD, A- to, toward
adhere, adjacent, adjunct, adroit, advent, abeyance, abet

AL, ALT- another
alias, alienate, inalienable, altruism

AM, AMI- love, friend
amorous, amicable, amiable, amity

AMBI, AMPHI- both
ambiguous, ambivalent, ambidextrous, amphibious

AMBL, AMBUL- walk
amble, ambulatory, somnambulist

ANN, ENN- year
annual, annuity, biennial, perennial

ANTE, ANT-before
antecedent, antediluvian, antebellum, anterior, antiquated, anticipate

ANTHROP- human
anthropology, anthropomorphic, misanthrope, philanthropy

ANTI, ANT- against, opposite
anticlimactic, antidote, antipathy, antithesis, antacid, antagonist, antonym

AUD- hear
audio, audience, audition, audible

AUTO- self
autobiography, autocrat, autonomous

BELLI, BELL- war
belligerent, bellicose, antebellum, rebellion

BENE, BEN- good
benevolent, benefactor, beneficent, benign

BI- two
bicycle, bisect, bilateral, bilingual, biped

BIBLIO- book
Bible, bibliography, bibliophile

BIO- life
biography, biology, amphibious, symbiotic, macrobiotic

BURS- money
reimburse, disburse, bursar, purse

CAP, CIP- head
captain, decapitate, capitulate, precipitous

CARN- flesh
carnal, carnage, carnivorous, incarnate

CED, CESS- yield, go
cease, cessation, incessant, cede, procession

CHROM- color
chrome, chromatic, monochrome

CHRON- time
chronology, chronic, anachronism

CIDE- murder
suicide, homicide, regicide, patricide

CIRCUM- around
circumference, circumnavigate, circumscribe, circumspect, circumvent

CLIN, CLIV- slope
incline, declivity, proclivity

CLUD, CLUS, CLAUS, CLOIS- shut, close
conclude, reclusive, claustrophobia, cloister, preclude, occlude

CO- with, together
coagulate, coalesce, coerce, cogent, cognate

COM- with, together
commensurate, compassion, compatriot, complacent, compliant, complicity

CON- with, together
conciliatory, concur, condone, conflagration, congeal, congenial, conglomerate, conjure, conjugal, conscientious, consecrate, consensus, constrained, contentious, convene, convivial, convoke, congress

COGN, GNO- know
recognize, cognition, cognizance, incognito, diagnosis, agnostic, prognosis, agnostic, ignorant

CONTRA- against
controversy, incontrovertible, contravene, contraindicate

CORP - body
corpse, corporeal, corpulence

COSMO, COSM- world
cosmopolitan, cosmos, microcosm, macrocosm

CRAC, CRAT - rule, power
democracy, bureaucracy, theocracy, autocrat, aristocrat, technocrat

CRED- trust, believe
incredible, credulous, credence, credentials

CRESC, CRET - grow

crescent, crescendo, accretion

CULP- blame, fault
culprit, culpable, inculpate, exculpate

CURR, CURS- run
current, concur, cursory, precursor, incursion

DE- down, out, apart
depart, debase, debilitate, decry, deface, defamatory, defunct, delegate, demean, demur, deplete, deplore, depravity, deprecate, deride, detest, devoid

DEC- ten, tenth
decade, decimal, decathlon, decimate

DEMO, DEM- people
democrat, demographics, demagogue, epidemic, pandemic, endemic

DIA- across
diagonal, diatribe, dialectic

DIC, DICT – speak, say
diction, interdict, predict, abdicate, indict, verdict, indicate, contradict

DIS- not, apart, away
disband, disburse, discern, discordant, disparate, dispassionate, dissemble, disseminate, dissension, dissipate, dissonant, dissuade, distend

DIF- apart, away
differentiate, diffidence, diffuse, digress

DOL- pain
condolence, doleful, dolorous, indolent

DUC, DUCT- lead
seduce, induce, conduct, viaduct, induct, ductile

DYS- abnormal, impaired
dyspeptic, dystrophy, dyslexia

EGO- self
ego, egoist, egocentric

EN, EM- in, into
enter, entice, encumber, endemic, ensconce, enthrall, entreat

EM- in, into
embellish, embezzle, embroil, empathy

EQUI – equal
equitable, equilateral, equinox, equilibrium

ERR- wander
erratic, aberration, errant

EU- well, good
eulogy, euphemism, euphony, euphoria, eurhythmics, euthanasia

EX- out, out of
exit, exacerbate, excerpt, excommunicate, exculpate, exhume, exonerate, exorbitant, exorcise, expatriate, expedient, expunge, extenuate, extort, extremity, extricate, extrinsic, exult

108

FAC, FIC, FECT - make, do
factory, facility, benefactor, malefactor, fiction, fictive, beneficent, affect, rectify

FAL, FALS- deceive
false, infallible, fallacious

FERV - boil
fervent, fervid, effervescent

FLU, FLUX- flow
fluent, flux, affluent, confluence, effluvia, superfluous

FORE- before
forecast, foreboding, forestall, forward

FRAG, FRAC- break
fragment, fracture, diffract, fractious, refract

FUS- pour
profuse, infusion, effusive, diffuse

GEN- class, kind
generation, congenital, homogeneous, heterogeneous, engender, progeny, generate, generic

GRAD- step
graduate, gradual, retrograde, centigrade, degrade, gradation, gradient

GRESS- step
progress, digress, transgress

GRAPH, GRAM- writing
biography, bibliography, epigraph, grammar, epigram

GRAT - pleasing
grateful, gratitude, gratis, ingrate, congratulate, gratuitous, gratuity

GRAV; GRIEV- heavy
grave, gravity, aggravate, grieve, aggrieve, grievous

GREG- crowd, flock
segregate, gregarious, egregious, congregate, aggregate

HABIT, HIBIT - have, hold
habit, inhibit, cohabit, habitat

HAP- by chance
happen, haphazard, hapless, mishap

HELI- sun
heliocentric, helium, heliotrope

HETERO- other
heterosexual, heterogeneous, heterodox

HOL- whole
holocaust, catholic, holistic

HOMO- same
homosexual, homogenize, homogeneous, homonym

HOMO- man
homo sapiens, homicide, bonhomie

HYDR- water
hydrant, hydrate, dehydration

HYPER- too much, excess
hyperactive, hyperbole, hyperventilate

HYPO- too little, under
hypodermic, hypothermia, hypochondria, hypothesis, hypothetical

IG – not
ignorant, ignoble, ignominious

IN- not
incorrigible, indelible, inept, inexorable, insatiable, insolvent, insomnia, interminable, intractable, incessant, infallible, infamy, inoperable, incandescent, indenture, ingratiate, introvert

IM - not
immaculate, immutable, impasse, impeccable, impertinent, implacable, impotent, impregnable, impervious

INTER- between, among
intercede, intercept, interject, interloper, intermediary, intermittent, interpolate, interpose, intersect, intervene

INTRA, INTR- within
intrastate, intravenous, intramural, intrinsic

IT, ITER- between, among
transit, itinerant, reiterate, transitory

JECT, JET- throw
eject, interject, abject, trajectory, jettison, projection

JOUR- day
journal, adjourn, sojourn

JUD- judge
judge, judicious, prejudice, adjudicate

JUNCT, JUG- join
junction, adjunct, injunction, conjugal, subjugate

JUR- swear, law
jury, abjure, adjure, conjure, perjure, jurisprudence

LAT - side
lateral, collateral, unilateral, bilateral, quadrilateral

LEG, LEC, LEX- read, speak
legible, lecture, lexicon

LEV- light
elevate, levitate, levity, alleviate

LIBER- free
liberty, liberal, libertarian, libertine

LING, LANG- tongue
lingo, language, linguistics, bilingual

LITER- letter
literate, alliteration, literal

LITH- stone
monolith, lithograph, megalith

LOC – place
dislocate, local

LOQU, LOCUT- speech, thought
eloquent, loquacious, colloquial, soliloquy, circumlocution, interlocutor, monologue, dialogue, eulogy,

LUC, LUM- light
lucid, illuminate, elucidate, translucent

MACRO- great
macrocosm, macrobiotics

MAG, MAJ, MAS, MAX- great
magnify, majesty, master, maximum, magnanimous, magnate, magnitude

MAL- bad
malady, maladroit, malevolent, malodorous

MAN- hand
manual, manuscript, emancipate, manifest, manufacture

MAR sea
submarine, marine, maritime

MATER, MATR- mother
maternal, matron, matrilineal

MEDI- middle
intermediary, medieval, mediate

MEGA- great
megaphone, megalomania, megalith

MEM, MEN- remember
memory, memento, memorabilia, reminisce

METER, METR, MENS- measure
meter, thermometer, perimeter, metronome, commensurate

MICRO- small
microscope, microorganism, microcosm, microbe

MIS- wrong, bad, hate
misunderstand, misanthrope, misapprehension, misconstrue, misnomer, mishap

MIT, MISS- send
transmit, emit, missive

MOLL- soft
mollify, emollient, mollusk

MON, MONIT- warn
admonish, monitor, premonition

MONO- one
monologue, monotonous, monogamy, monolith, monochrome, monopoly

MOR, MORT - dead
morbid, moribund, mortal, amortize

MORPH- shape
amorphous, metamorphosis, morphology

MULT – many
multitude, multifarious

MUT - change
mutate, mutability, immutable, commute

NAT, NASC- born
native, nativity, natal, neonate, innate, cognate, nascent, renaissance

NEG- not, deny
negative, abnegate, renege

NEO- new
neoclassical, neophyte, neologism, neonate

NIHIL- none, nothing
annihilation, nihilism

NOM, NYM- name
nominate, nomenclature, misnomer, ignominious, antonym, homonym, pseudonym, synonym, anonymity

NUMER- number
numeral, numerous, innumerable, enumerate

OB- against
obstruct, obdurate, obfuscate, obnoxious, obsequious, obstinate, obtrusive

OMNI- all
omnipresent, omnipotent, omniscient, omnivorous

ONER- burden
onerous, onus, exonerate

OPER- work
operate, cooperate, inoperable

PAC- peace
pacify, pacifist, pacific

PALP- feel
palpable, palpitation

PAN- all
panorama, panacea, panegyric, pandemic

PARA – beside
paranormal, paraphrase, paraprofessional

PATER, PATR- father
paternal, paternity, patriot, compatriot, expatriate, patrimony, patricide, patrician

PATH, PASS- feel, suffer
sympathy, antipathy, empathy, apathy, pathos, impassioned

PEC- money
pecuniary, impecunious

PEL, PULS- drive
compel, compelling, expel, propel, compulsion

PEN- almost
penultimate, penumbra

PEND, PENS- hang
pendant, pendulous, compendium, suspense, propensity

PER- through, by, for, throughout
perfunctory, permeable, perturbation, perusal

PER- against, destruction
perfidious, pernicious, perjure, permeate

PERI- around
perimeter, periphery, peripatetic, periscope

PET- seek, go toward
petition, impetus, impetuous, petulant, centripetal

PHIL- love
philosopher, philanderer, philanthropy, bibliophile, philology

PHOB- fear
phobia, claustrophobia, xenophobia

PHON- sound
phonograph, megaphone, euphony, phonetics, phonics

PLAC- calm, please
placate, implacable, placid, complacent

PLIC – fold or bend
complicate, implicate

PORT- carry
portable, deportment, rapport, import

POT- power
potential, potent, impotent, potentate, omnipotence

PRE- before
precede, precipitate, preclude, precocious, precursor, predilection, predisposition, preponderance, prepossessing, prescient, prejudice, predict, premonition

PRIM- first
prime, primary, primal, primeval, primordial

PRO- ahead, forth
proceed, proclivity, procrastinator, progenitor, progeny, prognosis, prologue, propel, proponent, propose, proscribe, protestation, provoke

PROTO- first
prototype, protagonist, protocol

PROX, PROP- near
approximate, propinquity, proximity

PSEUDO- false
pseudoscientific, pseudonym

PYR- fire
pyre, pyrotechnics, pyromania

QUAD, QUAR, QUAT-four
quadrilateral, quadrant, quadruped, quarter, quaternary

QUES, QUER, QUIS- question
quest, inquest, query, querulous, inquisitive

QUIE- quiet
disquiet, acquiesce, quiescent, requiem

RADI- branch
radius, radiate, radiant, eradicate

RECT, REG- straight, rule
rectangle, rectitude, rectify, regular

RETRO- backward
retrospective, retroactive, retrograde

RID, RIS- laugh
ridiculous, deride, derision

ROG- ask
interrogate, derogatory, abrogate, arrogant

RUPT - break
disrupt, interrupt, rupture

SACR, SANCT- holy
sacred, sacrilege, consecrate, sanctify, sanction, sacrosanct

SCRIB, SCRIPT - write
scribe, ascribe, circumscribe, inscribe, proscribe

SCRIPT- write
script, manuscript, describe, prescription

SE- apart, away
separate, segregate, secede, sedition

SEC, SECT, SEG- cut
sector, dissect, bisect, intersect, segment, secant

SED, SID- sit
sedate, sedentary, supersede, reside, residence,

SEM- seed, sow
seminar, seminal, disseminate

SEMI- half
semiliterate, semicolon, semifinal, semi-lunar

SEN- old
senior, senile, senescent

SENT, SENS- feel, think
sentiment, nonsense, assent, sentient, consensus, sensual

SEQU, SECU- follow
sequence, sequel, subsequent, obsequious, obsequy, non sequitur, consecutive

SIGN- mark, sign
signal, designation, assignation

114

SIM, SEM- similar, same
similar, semblance, dissemble, verisimilitude

SOL- sun
solar, parasol, solarium, solstice

SOL- alone
solo, solitude, soliloquy

SOMN- sleep
insomnia, somnolent, somnambulist

SON- sound
sonic, consonance, dissonance, assonance, resonate

SOPH- wisdom
philosopher, sophistry, sophisticated, sophomoric

SPEC, SPIC- see, look
spectator, circumspect, retrospective, perspective, prospect, conspicuous

SPER- hope
prosper, prosperous, despair, desperate

SPERS, SPAR- scatter
disperse, sparse, aspersion, disparate

SPIR- breathe
respire, inspire, spiritual, aspire, transpire

STRICT, STRING- bind
strict, stricture, constrict, stringent, astringent

STRUCT, STRU- build
structure, construe, obstruct

SUB- under
subconscious, subjugate, subliminal, subsequent, subterranean, subvert

SUMM- highest
summit, summary, consummate

SUPER, SUR- above
supervise, supercilious, supersede, superfluous, surfeit

SURGE, SURRECT - rise
surge, resurgent, insurgent, insurrection

SYN, SYM- together
synthesis, sympathy, synonym, synopsis, symposium, symbiosis

TACIT, TIC- silent
tacit, taciturn, reticent

TACT, TAG, TANG- touch
tact, tactile, contagious, tangent, tangential, tangible

TEN, TAIN- hold, reach
detention, tenable, tenacious, retain

TEND, TENS, TENT- stretch
intend, distend, tension, tensile, ostensible, contentious

115

TERM- end
terminal, terminate, interminable

TERR- earth, land
terrain, terrestrial, extraterrestrial, subterranean

TEST- witness
testify, attest, testimonial, testament, detest, protestation

THE- god
atheist, theology, theocracy

THERM- heat
thermometer, thermal, thermonuclear, hypothermia

TIM- fear, frightened
timid, intimidate, timorous

TOP- place
topic, topography, utopia

TORP- stiff, numb
torpedo, torpid, torpor

TORT- twist
distort, extort, tortuous

TOX- poison
toxic, toxin, intoxication

TRACT - draw
tractor, intractable, protract, attract, extract

TRANS- across, through
transport, transgress, transient, transitory, translucent, transmutation

TREM, TREP- shake
tremble, tremor, tremulous, trepidation, intrepid

TURB- shake
disturb, turbulent, perturbation

UMBR- shadow
umbrella, umbrage, adumbrate, penumbra

UNI, UN- one
unify, unilateral, unanimous, unique

URB- city
urban, suburban, urbane

VAC-empty
vacant, evacuate, vacuous

VAL- value, strength
valid, valor, convalescence

VAIL- value, strength
avail, prevail, countervail

VEN - come
convene, contravene, intervene, venue

VENT- come
convention, circumvent, advent, prevention

VER- true
verify, verity, verisimilitude, veracious, aver, verdict

VERB- word
verbal, verbose, verbiage, verbatim

VERT, VERS- turn
avert, convert, pervert, revert, incontrovertible, divert, subvert, versatile, aversion

VICT, VINC- conquer
victory, conviction, evict, evince, invincible

VID, VIS- see
evident, vision, visage, supervise

VIL- base, mean
vile, vilify, revile

VIV; VIT - life
vivid, vital, convivial, vivacious

VOC, VOK- call, word
vocal, equivocate, vociferous, convoke, evoke, invoke

VOL- wish
voluntary, malevolent, benevolent, volition

VOLV; VOLUT - turn, roll
revolve, evolve, convoluted

VOR- eat
devour, carnivore, omnivorous, voracious

Suffixes

Suffix	Meaning	Examples
able, ible	capable of	credible
ance, ence	state of	abundance
ant	full of	luxuriant
ate	one who	candidate
cy	position of	presidency
er, or	one who	singer
escent	becoming	adolescent
fic	making	traffic
fy	make	pacify
ia	disease	anemia
ion	act of	separation
ious	characterized by	spacious
ish	like	girlish
ism	belief	racism
ist	one who	activist
ive	relating to	passive
ize	to make	apologize
ness	quality of	aggressiveness
oid	like	humanoid
ology	study of	scientology
ose	full of	verbose
ous	full of	curious
tude	state of	attitude
ure	state of, act	stature

Appendix 2a. Practical Groupings of Commonly Tested Words

Pairs of Synonyms & Antonyms

Old: Archaic, hackneyed, medieval, obsolete

New: Innovative, nascent, novice

Hard Working: Assiduous, diligent, persevering, tenacious

Lazy: Apathetic, indolent, insipid, languid, lethargic, torpor

Short and Concise: Laconic, succinct, pithy, brevity, terse

Wordy: Verbose, circumlocution, redundant

Religious: Apotheosis, consecrate, divine, ethereal, hallow, rectitude, sacrosanct

Unholy / Non-Religious: Atheist, agnostic, desecrate

Sanctimonious: Smug, pious, self-righteous

Lively/ Active: Brisk, dynamic, ebullient, exuberant, scintillating, stimulating, titillating

Sad / Bleak: Dejected, forlorn, lackluster, lugubrious, melancholy, muted, somber, tenebrous

To Praise Someone: Acclaim, adulate, applaud, commend, eulogize, exalt, extol, flatter, hail, laud, panegyrize, tout

To Belittle, Insult or Scold Someone: Admonish, assail, berate, calumniate, castigate, censure, chastise, chide, decry, denigrate, deride, denounce, disparage, excoriate, execrate, lambaste, malign, rebuke, reprimand, reproach, scold, upbraid

Careful: Cautious, circumspect, conscientious, discreet, exacting, fastidious, gingerly, heedful, judicious, meticulous, prudent, punctilious, scrupulous, wary

Careless: Culpable, indifferent, insouciant, lackadaisical, lax, negligent, perfunctory, rash, remiss, reprehensible

Courageous: Audacious, dauntless, gallant, intrepid, stalwart, undaunted, valiant, valorous

Timid / Shy: Aloof, ascetic, demure, diffident, insular, indisposed, laconic, quiescent, reserved, reticent, subdued, taciturn, timorous

Humble: Demure, diffident, laconic, plebian, reticent, subdued, subservient, taciturn, timorous, unassuming, unpretentious, unostentatious

Arrogant : Audacious, condescending, disdainful, despotic, egotistical, flippant, haughty, imperious, impudent, insolent, ostentatious, patronizing, pompous, supercilious, superiority, turgid, vainglorious

Pleasant / Friendly: Affable, amenable, amiable, agreeable, congenial, cordial, decorous, ebullient, effervescent, engaging, gracious, gregarious, jocular, obliging

Unpleasant: Callous, cantankerous, captious, churlish, contentious, gruff, irascible, ornery, perverse, petulant, querulous, testy, vexing, wayward

To Make a Tense Situation Better: Abate, accede, accommodate, allay, ameliorate, appease, assuage, comply, concede, conciliate, mitigate, mollify, pacify, placate, propitiate, quell, salve, satiate

To Make a Tense Situation Worse: Alienate, antagonize, contradict, dispute, embitter, estrange, exacerbate, incense, infuriate, nettle, oppugn, oppose

Generous: Altruistic, beneficent, benevolent, charitable, effusive, humanitarian, magnanimous, munificent, philanthropic

Cheap: Frugal, miserly, paltry, parsimonious, penurious, provident, thrifty

Abundant or Rich: Affluent, bounteous, copious, luxuriant, multifarious, multitudinous, opulent, pecuniary, plenteous, plentiful, plethoric, prodigious, profuse, prosperous, replete, teeming, wealthy

Excessive, too much: Ebullience, effusive, egregious, flagrant, frenetic, gratuitous, opulent, superfluous

Scarce or Poor: Austere, bereft, dearth, deficit, destitute, impoverished, indigent, insolvent, meager, paltry, paucity, penurious, scarcity, sparse

To Comply or Negotiate: Accommodate, acquiesce, amenable, capitulate, compliant, deferential, malleable, pliant, obliging, submissive, subservient, tractable

Refusing to Give In: Adamant, immutable, indomitable, inflexible, intractable, intransigent, recalcitrant, relentless, steadfast, tenacious

Good communication: Clarity, cogent, coherent, cohesive, didactic, discourse, eloquence, fluid, lucid

Poor communication / Hard to understand: Convoluted, cryptic, futile, impede, obscure

Honorable, Strong Character: Assiduous, benevolent, decorous, diligent, fidelity, fortitude, intrepid, magnanimous

Poor Character: Effrontery, haughty, insolent, irascible, licentious, mendacious, mercurial, petulant, supercilious, truculent, vindictive, wanton

General / Neutral Words

Undecided: Ambivalent, equivocate, tenuous, unsure

Boring: Austere, mundane, dull, ordinary, commonplace, ponderous, prosaic

Calm (Emotionally): Decorous, equanimity, propriety, prudent, serene, staid, stoic

Intelligence / Intellectual: Acumen, arcane, astute, cognizant, didactic, erudite, esoteric, ingenious, perspicacious

Joining Together: Aggregate, coalesce, confluence, linchpin, yoke

Large / Spacious: Majestic, behemoth, commodious, grandiose, palatial, sublime

Time / History: Anachronistic, antecedent, antediluvian, chronological, dilatory, ephemeral, expedite, hiatus, prescient, portent, primeval, quotidian, transient

Arguing: Altercation, beseech, cajole, coerce, contentious

Proving a Point: Cogent, debunked, dogmatic, sophistry, persuasive, arbitrate

Uncertain or Cautious: Addled, ambiguous, amorphous, circumspect, dubious, equivocal, prudent, vacillate

Forgiveness: Absolve, atone, clemency, condone, exonerate,

Negative Character Traits

Rude: Brusque, caustic, fractious, incorrigible, ingrate, insolent, pugnacious

Evil: Abominable, depravity, enmity, heinous, malediction, malfeasance, malice, nefarious, putrid, rancorous

Hatred: Abhor, animosity, antipathy, enmity, malevolent, odious, wrath

Untruthful / Deceptive: Chicanery, dubious, dogmatic, devious, duplicity, fabricated, hypocrisy, prevaricate, slander, spurious, trickery, wily, unctuous

Sneaky: Astute, clever, cunning, clandestine: secretive, disingenuous, ruse, shrewd, stratagem

Greed / Envy: Avarice, cupidity, covet

To Harbor Bad Feelings: Harbinger, ominous, timorous, trepidation, apprehension

Odd or Abnormal: Aberration, atypical, eclectic, eccentric, iconoclast, idiosyncratic

Appendix 2b. 50 Common Antonym Pairs

Archaic: innovative
Obsolete: nascent
Diligent: indolent
Assiduous: apathetic
Laconic: verbose
Succinct: redundant
Tenacious: lethargic
Brevity: verbose
Ebullient: tenebrous
Dynamic: lugubrious

Scintillating: lackluster
Exalt: deride
Panegyrize: excoriate
Adulate: execrate
Extol: calumniate
Hail: chide
Punctilious: lackadaisical
Prudent: remiss
Stalwart: timorous
Intrepid: laconic

Audacious: quiescent
Ascetic: materialistic
Haughty: diffident
Amenable: captious
Jocular: cantankerous
Decorous: churlish
Engaging: contentious
Ameliorate: exacerbate
Propitiate: nettle
Quell: oppugn

Munificent: parsimonious
Benevolent: penurious
Opulent: paucity
Plethoric: exiguous
Effusive: dearth
Capitulate: intransigent
Pliant: immutable
Capricious: deliberate
Disingenuous: candid
Desecration: reverence

Cogent: cryptic
Lucid: convoluted
Mendacious: honest
Mercurial: steadfast
Yoke: cleave
Prosaic: imaginative
Stoic: effervescent
Cognizant: ignorant
Arcane: commonplace
Behemoth: infinitesimal

Appendix 3. Tricky Look-alike (and Sound-alike) Words

The following pairs of words are particular favorites of the GRE test writers. Why? Because they look alike, sound alike and are frequently confused by nervous students. A favorite trick of the test writers is to include the "wrong" word as a potential answer choice in the Antonym, Analogy, and Sentence Completion sections, when the real answer is its look-alike synonym.

See Chapter 2 for specific strategies for vocabulary challenges on the GRE. Also see Appendix 6 for a list of commonly confused *verbs* on the GRE.

adulate: to praise **adulterate**: to make impure

adverse: hostile **averse**: unwilling

allegory: symbolic work of literature **allegro**: quick, rapid

allude: to hint at or refer to   **elude:** to avoid

ambulance: emergency transport vehicle **ambulatory**: walking

anachronism: an outdated custom **anarchism**: disruptive

antipathy: hatred, aversion **apathy**: indifference **antithesis**: opposite

arcane: mysterious **archaic**: old-fashioned

aquiline: curved or hooked   **aquatic**: pertaining to water

artifact: a handmade object **artifice**: trick; deception

ascetic: self-denying, abstinent   **aseptic:** without bacteria **aesthetic**: beautiful, artistic

baleful: foreshadows evil **baneful**: poisonous, deadly   **banal**: trite

beseech: to beg   **besiege:** to overwhelm, move in on   **bestial**: savage, brutal

callous: insensitive   **callow**: young, inexperienced

censure: blame, criticize **censor**: to remove the inappropriate

capacious: roomy **capricious**: impulsive **captious**: hard to please

capitulate: to surrender   **recapitulate**: to repeat

circumspect: cautious **circumvent**: bypass **circumscribe**: to limit or confine

concave: hollow, curved inward   **conclave**: secret meeting **convex** curve outward

congenial: friendly **congenital**: existing at birth

contiguous: nearby, neighboring **contingent:** possible

covet: to desire   **covert**: hidden; secret   **covenant**: an agreement

delude: to deceive or mislead   **deluge**: a rush or flood

demur: to object **demure**: shy

denigrate: to ruin someone's character **delineate**: to portray or depict in writing

deprecate: to disapprove of   **depreciate:** to lessen in value

desecrate: to damage a holy place   **desiccate:** to dry

dilate: to expand   **dilatory:** slow or late

disparate: different, diverse,   **desperate:** needy, beyond reason

discreet: cautious, showing good judgment   **discrete:** separate, not attached

dissemble; to disguise one's character   **disassemble;** to take apart

dissident: disagreeing   **dissonant:** out of harmony

divers: several   **diverse:** distinct, varied

effluent: flowing out   **effulgent:** radiant

elicit: to draw out, provoke   **illicit:** illegal, improper

ephemeral: brief   **ethereal:** eerie or ghostly

epitaph: inscription on a tombstone   **epithet:** a descriptive word or phrase

exacerbate: to aggravate   **excoriate:** to criticize   **exonerate:** to free from blame

exculpate: to vindicate   **execrate:** to curse   **expatiate:** to expand upon

explicate: to explain   **expiate:** to atone for   **extirpate:** to destroy or remove

extricate: to set free, disentangle   **extrapolate:** to infer or estimate

fervid: emotional   **fervent:** eager, earnest

gorge: to overeat   **gouge** to overcharge

gratitude: thanks   **platitude:** cliche

heterogeneous: diverse throughout   **homogeneous:** the same throughout

ignoble: immoral   **noble:** honorable

illusion: something unreal deceptive   **allusion:** indirect reference

imbibe: to drink   **imbue:** to infuse, dye, wet or moisten

imminent: soon   **eminent:** famous   **immolate:** to kill by fire

imperious: domineering   **impervious:** hardened

impetus: a stimulus   **impetuous:** impulsive

impugn: to attack or challenge   **impunity:** freedom from punishment

incongruous: inappropriate   **incredulous:** skeptical

indigent: very poor   **indignant:** angry, insulted   **indigenous:** native, inborn

ingenious: original, clever   **ingenuous:** straightforward, open

indolent: lazy   **insolent:** rude

ingrate: ungrateful person **ingratiate**; to obtain someone's favor

inimical: harmful **inimitable**: unable to be imitated or equaled

inspired: encouraged **insipid**: bland or dull

mendicant: beggar **mendacious:** dishonest

pallid: pale or dull **palliate**: to ease or lessen

penury: extreme poverty **penurious**: stingy

pestilence: epidemic, plague **petulance**: irritable or ill-tempered

potent: strong **potable**: drinkable **potentate**: monarch or ruler

précis: brief summary **precipice**: cliff **precipitous**: very steep **precipitate**: sudden

precede: to come before **proceed**: to continue

prescribe: to order or advise **proscribe**: to outlaw

prodigal; wasteful **prodigious**: enormous, vast

qualitative: having to do with a quality, **quantitative**: having to do with a number

sanguine: cheerful, optimistic **sanguinary**: bloody

sardonic: scornful or mocking **sartorial**: pertaining to clothing

sentient: conscious, feeling **sentinel**: guard

soporific: causing sleep **sophomoric**: immature

solicit: to ask or seek **solicitude**: concern, anxiety

suffer: hurt **suffrage**: right to vote

tortuous: winding **torturous**: causing pain

vicious: mean **viscous**: sticky

waver: to fluctuate in thought or opinion **waiver:** giving up a claim

Appendix 4. 200 Commonly Tested Words (in Context)

ABERRANT: abnormal or deviant.

The drug caused ABERRANT behavior in otherwise normal patients.

ABSCOND: to leave secretly

Cheyenne ABSCONDED from McDonalds without paying her bill.

ABATE: to reduce in amount or severity

After the storm ABATED, people left the shelter and returned to their homes.

ABSTAIN: to choose not to do something

The priest will voluntarily ABSTAIN from sexual activity.

ABYSS: an extremely deep hole

The rodent scurried into his hiding place in the deep ABYSS of the cave.

ADULATE: to praise

The citizens greeted the generous plan with great ADULATION.

ADULTERATE: to make impure

The suspicious-tasting milk was ADULTERATED with water.

ADVOCATE: to speak in favor of

The physician ADVOCATED a lifestyle including rigorous exercise.

AESTHETIC: concerning beauty and appearance

Decorators include flowers in home decor for their AESTHETIC appeal.

AGGRANDIZE: to increase in power and influence

The overzealous job candidate AGGRANDIZED himself by claiming achievements beyond his ability.

ALLEVIATE: to make more bearable

Two ibuprofen tablets will ALLEVIATE the pain from a headache.

AMALGAMATE: to combine or mix together

When IBM and GE joined, they called their AMALGAMATED firm the Mega-Corporation.

AMBIGUOUS: doubtful or uncertain

Jane's AMBIGUOUS response to his marriage proposal made Joe doubt her sincerity.

AMELIORATE: to improve

Jane can AMELIORATE her dental pain by taking aspirin.

ANACHRONISM: something out of place in time

The 1950's music seemed ANACHRONISTIC in the modern nightclub.

ANARCHISM: disruptive

School administrators viewed the peace protest as pure ANARCHY.

ANALOGOUS: similar or alike in some way; equivalent to

My love for my son is ANALOGOUS to my father's love for me.

ANOMALY: deviation from what is normal

Her friendly behavior at the dance was an ANOMALOUS deviation from her usual frosty demeanor.

ANTAGONIZE: to annoy or provoke to anger

The child ANTAGONIZED the cat by pulling its tail.

ANITPATHY: extreme dislike

The ANTIPATHY between Clare and her mother-in-law often descended into verbal fighting.

APATHY: lack of interest or emotion

APATHETIC voters don't bother to show up at the polls.

ARBITRATE: to judge a dispute

Since the couple could not agree on a property settlement, a judge was forced to ARBITRATE their divorce proceedings.

ARCHAIC: ancient, old-fashioned

Her ARCHAIC computer could not handle the latest software.

ARDOR: intense and passionate feeling

Jason's ARDOR for Joan was evident when he passionately described her beauty.

ARDUOUS: hard or strenuous

Moving the heavy furniture was an ARDUOUS task.

ARTICULATE: able to speak clearly and expressively

His ARTICULATE defense of his client convinced the jury to acquit him of all charges.

ASSUAGE: to make something unpleasant less severe

Paula used overeating to ASSUAGE her sense of meaninglessness and despair.

ATTENUATE: to weaken

The new law ATTENUATED the government's power to arrest people for frivolous reasons.

AUDACIOUS: fearless and daring

The AUDACIOUS waitress insulted her customer, with no fear of possible reprisal.

AUSTERE: plain, undecorated

The nuns' AUSTERE home was completely unadorned.

BANAL: predictable, boring

Flight attendants greet all passengers with BANAL phrases like "Have a nice day."

BANEFUL: poisonous, deadly

The snake's venom, which killed its victims within minutes, was unusually BANEFUL.

BOLSTER: to support; to prop up

The metal brackets BOLSTERED the heavy bookshelves onto the wall.

BOMBASTIC: pompous in speech and manner

Jake's BOMBASTIC claims were too outrageous to be believed.

BURGEON: to grow

Engineering was a BURGEONING field in the 1980's, when companies began to go "high tech."

CACOPHONY: harsh, jarring noise

The chirping of the birds created a CACOPHONY in the normally silent backyard.

CANDID: impartial and honest

Children's observations are usually CANDID and unpretentious.

CAPRICIOUS: fickle

Jill's CAPRICIOUS nature led her to change boyfriends quite often.

CASTIGATE: to punish or criticize harshly

European countries CASTIGATE perpetrators for crimes that are considered minor in the United States.

CATALYST: something that brings about a change in something else

Jack's great job on the project was the CATALYST that led to his promotion.

CAUSTIC: biting in wit

Jim's insulting, yet clever remarks gave him a reputation for CAUSTIC wit.

CHAOS: great disorder or confusion

Without proper supervision, the children's behavior will descend into CHAOS.

CHAUVINISM: blind devotion to a group or cause

Male CHAUVINISTS think that men are inherently superior to women.

CHICANERY: deception or trickery

Dishonest salesmen often use CHICANERY to sell their least desirable products.

COGENT: convincing and well reasoned

Swayed by the COGENT argument of the defense, the jury acquitted the defendant.

COMPENDIUM: a brief summary

Most students read the COMPENDIUM, rather than the entire text.

CONDONE: to overlook or disregard

Failing to prosecute minor crimes CONDONES lawlessness.

CONVOLUTED: intricate, complicated

Rather than tell the truth, Jane made up a long, CONVOLUTED story to explain her absence.

CORROBORATE: to provide supporting evidence

Physical evidence CORROBORATED the witness's testimony.

CRAVEN: cowardly

A CRAVEN man refuses to stand up for his beliefs,

CREDULOUS: too trusting, gullible

Only CREDULOUS 9-year-olds still believe in Santa Claus.

CRESCENDO: steadily increasing

The CRESCENDO of tension became unbearable as the mystery movie continued.

DECORUM: appropriateness of behavior or conduct

The biker lacked the DECORUM appropriate for a formal dinner.

DEFERENCE: respect, courtesy

Gentle George treated his elderly grandmother with the utmost DEFERENCE.

DERIDE: to mock

The haughty teenagers DERIDED their awkward peers.

DESICCATE: to dry thoroughly

DESICCATED coconut has been dried and browned in a hot oven.

DESECRATE: to damage a holy place

The enemy's attack completed DESECRATED the ancient temple.

DIATRIBE: an abusive, condemnatory speech

The angry husband bellowed a DIATRIBE at his unsuspecting wife.

DESULTORY: jumping from one to another; disconnected

Jade had a DESULTORY education, dropping out at the drop of a hat.

DIFFIDENT: shy; lacking self-confidence

Sara's DIFFIDENT manner during her date suggested she was not interested in Jake.

DILATE: to expand

My pupils DILATE when I enter a dark room.

DILATORY: intended to delay

The attorney used DILATORY means to stall the trial.

DILETTANTE: someone with a superficial interest in a topic

DILETTANTES have only a superficial interest in the hobby.

DIRGE: a funeral hymn or mournful speech

Mike wrote a DIRGE for the funeral of his cherished grandfather.

DISABUSE: to set right or free from error

To DISABUSE his critics, the scientist repeated his experiments.

DISCERN: to perceive or recognize

It is not always easy to DISCERN the difference between genuine pieces and imitations.

DISPARATE: different; unlike

The boys look alike, yet their personalities are DISPARATE.

DISSEMBLE: to present a false appearance; to disguise one's real intentions or character

The lying husband could DISSEMBLE to his wife no longer; he admitted his plans to leave her.

DISSONANCE: a harsh and disagreeable combination

The speaker's unpopular views caused considerable DISSONANCE in the audience.

DOGMA: a firmly held opinion, often a religious belief

Karen's firm DOGMA was that our souls all live multiple lives through reincarnation.

DUPE: to deceive; a person who is easily deceived

Con artists often DUPE the elderly out of their life savings.

EBULLIENT: highly enthusiastic

The bride was EBULLIENT at her long-awaited wedding.

ECLECTIC: from a variety of sources

Jade's furniture is an ECLECTIC mix of modern and southwestern styles.

EFFICACY: effectiveness

The EFFICACY of the drug is reduced if it is not taken according to the directions.

ELEGY: a sorrowful poem or speech

The author wrote an emotional ELEGY about his mother's death.

ELOQUENT: persuasive and moving speech

The President gave an ELOQUENT speech in honor of the lost soldiers.

EMULATE: to copy; to try to equal or exceed

Jody tried to EMULATE her older sister Connie, copying her dress, hairstyle and mannerisms.

ENERVATE: to reduce in strength

The US military's surprise attacks ENERVATED the opposing army.

ENGENDER: to produce, cause, or bring about

Laura's fear of dogs was ENGENDERED at age six, when she was bitten by a pit bull.

ENIGMA: a puzzle or mystery

Lois was so quiet about her personal life that she was somewhat of an ENIGMA in the otherwise close group.

ENUMERATE: to count, list, or itemize

The wife ENUMERATED her husband's faults during their bitter argument.

EPHEMERAL: lasting a short time

The heady romantic phase of a relationship is EPHEMERAL in the context of a lifelong marriage.

EQUIVOCATE: to mislead by using expressions of double meaning

The witness EQUIVOCATED when questioned by the police, misleading them about the time of the robbery.

ERRATIC: wandering and unpredictable

The excited puppy ran ERRATICALLY through the house, often bumping into the furniture.

ERUDITE: learned, scholarly

The annual research meeting attracted the most ERUDITE, well-published individuals.

ESOTERIC: known or understood by only a few

The teacher struggled to explain the ESOTERIC world of forensic science to the young class.

ESTIMABLE: admirable

Diane's commitment to charity work is ESTIMABLE, considering her busy schedule.

EULOGY: a speech that praises someone

David gave his father's EULOGY; outlining his achievements and delightful personality.

EUPHEMISM: an inoffensive word that is used in place of a distasteful one

The human resource director preferred to use the EUPHEMISM "outsourced" instead of "fired."

EXACERBATE: to make worse

Karen's fever was EXACERBATED by her new infection.

EXCULPATE: to prove innocent

The defense attorney was hired to EXCULPATE his innocent client.

EXIGENT: urgent

Because the bank robbers had weapons, it was EXIGENT for the police to capture them.

EXONERATE: to clear of blame

Mr. Williams was EXONERATED when his partner confessed to stealing the money.

EXPLICIT: clearly stated or shown

The homeowners left a list of EXPLICIT instructions for their housecleaner to follow.

EXTRICATE; to set free, disentangle

When she realized she was in danger, Jan EXTRICATED herself from the situation.

EXTRAPOLATE: to infer or estimate

The statistician EXTRAPOLATED his data from a small sample to the entire population.

FANATICAL: excessively enthusiastic or devoted

The moviegoers were FANATICAL in their devotion to Tom Cruise, praising even his worst movies.

FATUOUS: foolish and smug

Feminists scoff at traditional beliefs, which they believe to be FATUOUS.

FAWN: to grovel

Diane FAWNED over the stagehand, hoping to gain a backstage pass for the concert.

FERVID: intensely emotional

Beatles fans were FERVID, doing anything to catch a glimpse of the group.

FLORID: excessively decorated

Having more money than taste, the lottery winner decorated her home in an excessively FLORID style.

FOMENT: to arouse or incite

The candidate tried to FOMENT sentiment against the war during his impassioned speech.

FRUGALITY: a tendency to be thrifty or cheap

Due to Claire's FRUGALITY, she was able to save more than half of her take-home pay.

GARRULOUS: talkative

Jake loved GARRULOUS women, whose continuous talking allowed him to simply listen.

GREGARIOUS: outgoing, sociable

Friends loved to go out with Jill, who was always GREGARIOUS and friendly.

GUILE: deceit or trickery

The desperate soldier resorted to GUILE in an effort to trap his enemy.

GULLIBLE: easily deceived

The con man fooled GULLIBLE elderly people into investing their life savings.

HOMOGENOUS: of a similar kind

The group was fairly HOMOGENOUS, including seven food science majors.

ICONOCLAST: one who opposes established beliefs and customs

Because he rejected traditional beliefs, Jerry Garcia was considered an ICONOCLAST.

IMPERTURBABLE: not capable of being disturbed

The day care worker seemed IMPERTURBABLE, even when faced with the wildest tantrums.

IMPERVIOUS: impossible to penetrate

A good roof is IMPERVIOUS to moisture.

IMPETUOUS: quick to act without thinking.

Rachel preferred to think through her options thoroughly, rather than make an IMPETUOUS move.

IMPLACABLE: unable to be calmed down or made peaceful

John's rage at his wife's betrayal left him IMPLACABLE for weeks.

INCHOATE: not fully formed; disorganized

In his first rough manuscript, the author's ideas were still INCHOATE.

INGENUOUS: showing innocence or childlike simplicity

Diane was INGENUOUS by nature, trusting everyone with the innocence of a child.

INIMICAL: hostile, unfriendly

Despite settling their lawsuit, the two sides were still INIMICAL to each other.

INNOCUOUS: harmless

Most bacteria are INNOCUOUS and pose no danger to humans.

INSIPID: lacking interest or flavor

INSIPID writing lacks interest and flavor.

INSULAR: isolated, narrow-minded

In Jenny's INSULAR hometown, most residents distrusted outsiders.

INTRANSIGENT: uncompromising

Joe's boss was INTRANSIGENT on the deadline, insisting that the project be completed on time.

INUNDATE: to overwhelm

After the hurricane, the insurance company was INUNDATED with claims.

IRASCIBLE: easily made angry

Dave's IRASCIBLE nature made it hard to keep friends and lovers.

LACONIC: using few words

Laura was a LACONIC speaker who used words as sparingly as possible.

LAMENT: to express sorrow; to grieve

Mara continues to LAMENT the death of her mother.

LAUD: to give praise; to glorify

The students LAUDED the success of Mr. Stevens, who was named Teacher of the Year.

LETHARGIC: acting in a slow, sluggish manner

The effects of mono left Grace so LETHARGIC that she couldn't complete her chores.

LOQUACIOUS: talkative

Her LOQUACIOUS nature was a problem at times when listening was more important than talking.

LUCID: clear and easily understood

The explanations were written in a simple and LUCID manner that readers easily understood.

LUMINOUS: bright, brilliant, glowing

The beach was bathed in LUMINOUS sunshine all summer long.

MALINGER: to evade responsibility by pretending to be ill

John hoped that his MALINGERING would prevent him from being drafted.

MALLEABLE: capable of being shaped

MALLEABLE precious metals can easily be formed into almost any shape.

MENDACIOUS: dishonest

Because Joe was MENDACIOUS, his wife did not believe anything he said.

METAPHOR: a figure of speech comparing two different things; a symbol

The METAPHOR "a sea of troubles" suggests a lot of troubles by comparing their number to the vastness of the sea.

METICULOUS: extremely careful about details

The investigators METICULOUSLY examined every inch of the crime scene.

MISANTHROPE: a person who dislikes others

Scrooge is such a MISANTHROPE that even children make him angry.

MITIGATE: to soften; to lessen

The storm MITIGATED after several hours, allowing stranded motorists to resume their journey home.

MOLLIFY: to calm or make less severe

The sparring spouses were so angry that no compromise would MOLLIFY them.

MONOTONY: lack of variation

The MONOTONY of the simple task drove the factory worker crazy.

MUNDANE: everyday

The strangers discussed MUNDANE matters while they waited for the bus.

OBDURATE: hardened in feeling; stubborn.

Monica was OBDURATE on the issue, and no amount of persuasion would change her mind.

OBSEQUIOUS: overly submissive; eager to please

The OBSEQUIOUS new secretary complimented her supervisors to the point of embarrassment.

OBSTINATE: stubborn, unyielding

The OBSTINATE child refused to eat any food that she disliked.

OBVIATE: to prevent; to make unnecessary

The unexpected bonus check OBVIATED her need for an emergency loan.

OCCLUDE: to stop up; to prevent the passage of

During a solar eclipse, the moon OCCLUDES the light from the sun.

ONEROUS: troublesome and oppressive; burdensome

The huge assignment was an ONEROUS burden to the already overworked team.

OPAQUE: impossible to see through; preventing the passage of light

The windows were almost OPAQUE from the buildup of dirt.

OPPROBRIUM: public disgrace

After his torrid extramarital affair became public, the Governor resigned in OPPROBRIUM.

OSTENTATION: excessive showiness

The King's palace was over-decorated in a dramatic, OSTENTATIOUS manner.

PALLIATIVE; to ease or lessen

The hospice offered PALLIATIVE care to ease the pain of cancer patients.

PARADOX: a contradiction or dilemma

In a sad PARADOX, those most in need of medical attention are least able to obtain it.

PARAGON: model of excellence or perfection

Miss America is the PARAGON of what a young woman should be: beautiful, intelligent, talented and fit.

PEDANT: someone who shows off learning

The professor's excessive commentary on the topic gained him a reputation as a PEDANT.

PERFIDIOUS: disloyal

The actress's PERFIDIOUS boyfriend revealed all of her intimate secrets to the press.

PERFUNCTORY: done in a routine way; indifferent

The harried waitress took the order and gave the waiting customer a PERFUNCTORY smile.

PHILANTHROPY: charity; a desire or effort to promote goodness

Charities owe most of their working capital to the PHILANTHROPY of private citizens in the community.

PLACATE: to soothe or pacify

The burglar tried to PLACATE the snarling dog by offering it a treat.

PLETHORA: excess

The house was overrun with a PLETHORA of knickknacks.

PRAGMATIC: practical

PRAGMATIC people realize that they will never win the lottery.

PRECIPITATE: to bring about abruptly

The revelation of Cassie's extramarital affair PRECIPITATED her divorce.

PRECIPITOUS: steep

The PRECIPITOUS hills of Colorado intimidated the novice hiker.

PREVARICATE: to lie

Rather than admit the truth, the employee PREVARICATED to avoid being chastised.

PRISTINE: fresh and clean

Jane cleaned all day so that Bob would return to a PRISTINE house.

PRODIGAL: lavish, wasteful

The PRODIGAL son wasted his inheritance on a decadent lifestyle.

PROLIFERATE: to increase in number quickly

The two hamsters quickly PROLIFERATED to several dozen.

PROPITIATE: to conciliate; to appease

Management PROPITIATED the irate union by agreeing to raise wages.

PROPRIETY: correct behavior; obedience

My grandmother maintained a high level of PROPRIETY, adhering to dozens of social rules.

PRUDENCE: wisdom, caution, or restraint

The college student exhibited PRUDENCE by carefully managing her small savings.

PUNGENT: sharp and irritating to the senses

The smoke from the burning casserole was extremely PUNGENT

QUIESCENT: motionless

QUIESCENT animals minimize their activity to conserve energy.

RAREFY: to make thinner or sparser

Because the atmosphere RAREFIES as altitudes increase, the air at the top of very tall mountains is too thin to breathe.

REPUDIATE: to reject the validity of

The woman's paternity suit was REPUDIATED when DNA tests showed her ex-boyfriend was not the father of her baby.

RETICENT: silent, reserved

RETICENT in her speech, Clara often remains unnoticed.

RHETORIC: effective writing or speaking

Lincoln's talent for RHETORIC was evident in his Gettysburg Address.

SANGUINE; cheerful, optimistic

Despite the devastating hurricane, the community remained SANGUINE about the future.

SARDONIC; scornful or mocking

The audience was insulted by the comedian's use of SARDONIC humor.

SATIATE: to satisfy fully or overindulge

His desire for power was so great that nothing could SATIATE it.

SOPORIFIC: causing sleep or lethargy

The SOPORIFIC movie left most viewers sleepy.

SPECIOUS: intentionally misleading

Jill's SPECIOUS excuse sounded legitimate, but was proved otherwise when her teacher called her home.

STIGMA: a mark of shame or discredit

As progressive as we seem, there is still a STIGMA against single motherhood.

STOLID: unemotional; lacking sensitivity

The convict appeared STOLID and unaffected by the judge's harsh sentence.

SUBLIME: lofty or grand

The SUBLIME music transformed the ordinary surroundings into a special place.

SUPERSEDE: to replace something or make it obsolete

Email messages SUPERSEDE faxes, which were expensive and wasteful.

TACITURN: silent, not talkative

John's father was so TACITURN that he rarely spoke to his own children.

TIRADE: verbal attack

Diane was shocked at her boss's TIRADE over such a minor mistake.

TORPOR: extreme sluggishness

After surgery, the patient experienced TORPOR until the anesthesia wore off.

TORTUOUS; winding

The long, TORTUOUS road included several dangerous curves.

TRANSITORY: temporary, lasting a brief time

The student lived a TRANSITORY life, moving almost every semester.

TRUCULENT: aggressive

The lion's TRUCULENCE inspired fear in others.

VACILLATE: to waver

The customer VACILLATED between ordering chocolate chip or rocky road ice cream.

VENERATE: to respect deeply

In China, the young VENERATE their elders, deferring to their wisdom and experience.

VERACITY: filled with truth and accuracy

The doctor's reputation for VERACITY made everyone trusted her description of events.

VEX: to annoy

The quiet old man was VEXED by his neighbor's loud music.

VOLATILE: easily aroused or changeable; lively or explosive

Fawn's VOLATILE personality made it hard to predict her reaction to anything.

WAVER: to fluctuate between choices

Dave WAVERED between asking Cathy and Sharon to the dance.

WHIMSICAL: acting in a fanciful or capricious manner; unpredictable

The WHIMSICAL ballet delighted the children with its imaginative characters.

ZEPHYR: gentle breeze

The ZEPHYR brought a feeling of coolness to the room.

Appendix 5. Grammar Review for the GRE™

Verb Tenses

The English language has the following verb tenses:

Present: Karen *walks* seven miles per day.
Present Perfect: Karen *has been walking* seven miles per day.
Present Progressive: Karen *is walking* seven miles per day.
Present Perfect Progressive: Karen *had been walking* seven miles per day.

Past: Karen *walked* seven miles per day.
Past Perfect: Karen *had walked* seven miles per day.
Past Progressive: Karen *was walking* seven miles per day.
Past Perfect Progressive: Karen *had been walking* seven miles per day.

Future: Karen *will walk* seven miles per day.
Future Perfect: Karen *will have walked* seven miles per day.
Future Progressive: Karen *will be walking* seven miles per day.
Future Perfect Progressive: Karen *will have been walking* seven miles per day.

Present Tense: is used to express:

a) *the present*: Sam *studies* all the time.
b) *general truths*: During times of war time, people *are* more patriotic.
c) *the future*: She *will go* to Europe next summer.

Past Tense: is used to express the past: She *went* to Europe last summer.

Past Participle: is used to form the:

a) *present perfect tense*, indicating that an action was started in the past and its effects are continuing in the present.

> She *has prepared* thoroughly for her trip to Europe.

b) *past perfect tense*, which indicates that an action was completed before another action.

> She *had prepared* thoroughly for her trip to Europe.

c) *future perfect tense*, which indicates that an action will be completed before another future action.
> She *will have prepared* thoroughly before traveling to Europe.

Present Participle (-ing forms of verbs): is used to form the **progressive tenses**:

a) *present progressive tense*, which indicates that an action is ongoing.

> She *is preparing* thoroughly for her trip to Europe.

b) *past progressive tense*, which indicates that an action was in progress in the past.

> She *was preparing* for her trip to Europe.

c) *future progressive tense*, which indicates that an action will be in progress in the future.

She *will be preparing* thoroughly for her trip to Europe.

Passive Verb Tense (or "Passive Voice"): The passive voice removes the subject from the sentence by combining the verb "to be" and the past participle of the main verb. The active voice is *always preferred*.

Passive	*Active*
A decision was made	The group made a decision
A house was sold	The realtor sold a house
A mistake was made	The student made a mistake
A good time was had by all	We all had a good time

Don't worry about naming the different verb tenses; the GRE will not ask you that. Instead, the writers will test your ability to:

- use the correct verb tense
- identify (and fix) errors in subject and verb agreement in sentences and paragraphs.

Subject & Verb Agreement

1. The subject and verb must agree in number and person.

Both of the following sentences are correct:

> We have surpassed our wildest expectations (plural)
> She has surpassed her wildest expectations. (singular)

2. Intervening phrases and clauses do not affect the subject-verb agreement.

Correct: Only one of the classes was cancelled.
Incorrect: Only one of the classes were cancelled.

The subject "one" is singular and requires a singular verb. The intervening phrase "of the classes" does not alter the number or person of the verb.

3. When the subject and verb are reversed, they must still agree in both number and person.

Both of the following sentences are correct:

> Attached are copies of my travel receipts.
> Copies of my receipts are attached.

Pronouns

A pronoun is a word that stands for a noun, known as the antecedent of the pronoun. Pronouns must agree with their antecedent in both number (singular or plural) and person (1st, 2nd, 3rd, etc.).

Example: Karen is waiting to pick up her dry cleaning.

The pronoun *her* refers to the noun Karen.

The most common pronouns in standard English include:

Singular:

I, me	she, her	he, him	it	anyone	either
each	many a	nothing	one	another	everything
mine	his, hers this	that			

Plural:

we, us	they	them	these	those	some
that	both	ourselves	any	many	few
several	others				

Both Singular and Plural:

any	none	all	most	more	who
which	what	you			

Basic Pronoun Rules:

1. Pronouns should be singular when they refer to one noun and plural when they refer to nouns joined by *and*.

Example: Rick and Amy believe they won the lottery.

The plural pronoun *they* refers to the compound subject "Rick and Amy."

2. A pronoun should be singular when it refers to two nouns joined by *or* or *nor*.

Correct: Neither Rita nor Amy believes she won the lottery.
Incorrect: Neither Rita nor Amy believes they won the lottery.

3. A pronoun should refer to one (and only one) noun or compound noun. This is the most common error in test questions. If a pronoun follows two nouns, it is often unclear which of the nouns the pronoun refers to.

Incorrect: The destabilization of the economy has left unstable stocks in the hands of frightened investors. It is imperative that they be more tightly controlled.

Should the unstable stocks be controlled or the frightened investors? Either interpretation is possible from the structure of the sentence.

Correct: The destabilization of the economy has left unstable stocks in the hands of frightened investors. It is imperative that the unstable stocks be more tightly controlled.

Incorrect: In Europe, they use perfume judiciously.

This construction is incorrect because the pronoun does not have an antecedent. The sentence needs a noun, rather than a pronoun.

Correct: In Europe, women use perfume judiciously.
Correct: European women use perfume judiciously.

4. A pronoun must also agree with its antecedent in person.

Incorrect: One enters the university with no friends. Then comes the stress of classes, choosing a major and qualifying for financial aid. No wonder you long to quit school!

The subject of the sentence changed from *one* (third person) to *you* (second person).

Correct: One enters the university with no friends. Then comes the stress of classes, choosing a major and qualifying for financial aid. No wonder one longs to quit school!

Correct: You enter the university with no friends. Then comes the stress of classes, choosing a major and qualifying for financial aid. No wonder you long to quit school!

Modifiers

1. A modifier should be placed as close as possible to the word (or phrase) it modifies.

Incorrect: Following are some useful tips for protecting your home from the police.
Correct: Following are some useful tips from the police for protecting your home.

In the first statement, the placement of the modifier implies that the police are a threat to your home.

2. When a phrase begins a sentence, make sure it modifies the subject of the sentence.

Incorrect: Coming from the mall, a few houses with Christmas lights caught my eye.
Correct: Coming from the mall, I saw Christmas lights on a few houses.

Parallelism

1. When two adjectives modify the same noun, they should have similar forms.

Incorrect: The exercise program was rigorous and a challenge.
Correct: The exercise program was rigorous and challenging.

2. When a series of clauses is listed, the verbs in each clause must have the same form.

Incorrect: During her trip to Acapulco, Jade will talk to the hotel about job opportunities, offer to work for minimum wage and trying to learn how to speak Spanish.

Correct: During her trip to Acapulco, Jade will talk to the hotel about job opportunities, offer to work for minimum wage and try to learn how to speak Spanish.

3. Both halves of a sentence should have the same structure.

Incorrect: To acknowledge Divine wisdom is taking the first step to nirvana.

Correct: Acknowledging Divine wisdom is taking the first step to nirvana.
Correct: To acknowledge Divine wisdom is to take the first step to nirvana.

Appendix 6. Errors in Word Usage Commonly Tested on the GRE™

The test writers tend to include the same idiom and usage errors on every exam. Here are the concepts that are tested most often.

Words and Phrases that are Always Incorrect

The words and phrases in the left column, although popular in spoken English, are **always wrong.** They should be replaced with the correct word or phrase in the right column:

Incorrect	Correct
Alot	A lot
Ain't	Isn't or aren't
Anyways	Anyway
Being that	Since, because
But that	That
As to whether	Whether
Can't hardly	Can hardly
Center around	Center
Conform with	Conform to
Consensus of opinion	Consensus
Could of, might of, must of	Could have, might have, must have
Different than	Different from
Doubt whether	Doubt that
Equally as good	As good, just as good
Enthuse	Enthusiastic
Identical to	Identical with
Independent from	Independent of
In contrast of	In contrast to
In regards to	In regard to, with regard to
Irregardless	Regardless
Kind of, sort of	Quite or somewhat
Not only...... and	Not only.... but also
Off of	Off
On account of	Because
Retroactive from	Retroactive to
The fact that	Because
The reason is because	The reason why
Where's it at?	Where is it?
Scarcely nothing	Scarcely anything

Commonly Confused Words and Phrases

All ready / Already: All ready means "everything is ready," while already means "earlier."

> The supplies are *all ready* to be packed in their boxes.
> Susan *already* visited the mall.

Among / Between: "Between" should be used when referring to two things, and "among" should be used when referring to more than two things.

> The bride must choose *between* two gorgeous gowns.
> The guilt is spread evenly *among* the three thieves.

Beside / Besides: Adding an "s" to beside completely changes its meaning. Beside means "next to," while besides means "in addition."

> Jill sat *beside* (next to) Kyle at the movie.
> *Besides* (in addition), the salary offered was less than desirable.

Disinterested / Uninterested: *Disinterested* means objective or unbiased, while *uninterested* means not caring about something.

> The feuding spouses sought advice from a *disinterested* third party.
> Jane was *uninterested* in Joe's story about catching fish.

Eminent / Imminent: *Eminent* means prominent or successful; *Imminent* means something will happen soon.

> An *eminent* surgeon performed dad's operation.
> After 9 months of pregnancy, the baby's arrival was *imminent.*

Farther / Further: Use farther when referring to distance, and use further when referring to degree.

> Shawn drove *farther* than Dave to reach the picnic.
> They went no *further* than making veiled threats.

Formerly / Formally: *Formerly* means previously; *formally* means officially.

> Janet's mother *formerly* lived in Seattle.
> Jennifer made the announcement *formally* on Friday.

Fewer / Less: Use *fewer* when referring to a number of items. Use *less* when referring to a continuous quantity.

> We had *fewer* choices for lunch.
> The cost was *less* than I expected.

Incite / Insight: Incite means *to instigate*; insight means *perception*.

> The leader's speech *incited* a riot.
> I appreciated Dave's *insight* about the problem in accounting.

Irrelevant / Irreverent: *Irrelevant* means unrelated; irreverent means *disrespectful.*

Focus on the main point, not the *irrelevant* details.
Diana was offended by the comic's *irreverent* sense of humor.

One another / Each other: *Each other* should be used when referring to two things, while *one another* should be used when referring to more than two things.

The six cast members congratulated *one another* on opening night.
Bridget and Carla congratulated *each other* on their college acceptances.

Perspective / Prospective: *Perspective* means viewpoint, while *prospective* means likely.

From Dan's *perspective,* the party was a huge mistake.
The realtor showed the house to a *prospective* buyer.

Regard / Regards: Unless giving best wishes to someone, use regard.

Incorrect: In *regards* to your request, we are happy to comply.
Correct: In regard to your letter, we are happy to comply.

Respectfully / Respectively: *Respectfully* means with respect, while *respectively* means in the order given.

Carla *respectfully* offered her resignation.
The first three letters in the alphabet are A, B, and C, *respectively.*

Whether / If: *Whether* introduces a choice, while *if* introduces a condition.

A common mistake is to use *if* to present a choice.

Incorrect: He asked *if* we wanted to accompany him.
Correct: He asked *whether* we wanted to accompany him.

The Most Commonly Misused Verbs on the GRE

Accept / Except: Accept means "to agree to" or "to receive," while except means "to object to" or "to leave out."

> We will *accept* your manuscript for review.
> No parking is allowed, *except* on holidays.

Account for:

When explaining something, the correct idiom is *account for*.
> We had to *account for* all of the missing money.

When receiving blame or credit, the correct idiom is *account to*:
> You will have to *account to* the state for your crimes.

Adapt / Adept / Adopt: Adapt means "to change," adept means "skilled," while adopt means "to make something your own."

> Eventually, Julie will *adapt* to her new environment.
> After years of practice, Ken is *adept* at algebra.
> We *adopted* a baby girl from China.

Adapted to / for / from:

Adapted to means "naturally suited for."
> The flamingo has *adapted to* the tropical temperatures.

Adapted for means "created to be suited for."
> For directives to succeed, they must be *adapted for* the continually changing economy.

Adapted from means "changed to be suited for."
> Billy Joel's' latest release is *adapted from* the 1993 soundtrack from *Cats*.

Affect / Effect:

Effect is a noun meaning "a result."
> Increased spending money will be the *effect* of the proposed tax decrease.

Affect is a verb meaning "to influence."
> The accident *affected* their plans for a leisurely drive.

Afflict / Inflict

Afflict means to suffer from a painful condition.
> My grandmother's hands are *afflicted* with arthritis.

Inflict means to punish someone.
> The judge *inflicted* a severe penalty for violating the law.

Affront / Confront: Affront means "to insult," while confront means "to face."

> Jane was *affronted* by her detractor's claims.
> Kevin *confronted* his fears head-on.

Apprise / Appraise: Apprise means "to inform," while apprise means "to determine the value" of something.

> The doctor *apprised* dad of mom's condition.
> The realtor *appraised* the house at one million dollars.

Collaborate / Corroborate: collaborate means "to work together," while corroborate means "to confirm" something.

> Jeff and Diane *collaborated* on a project for school.
> The witness *corroborated* the defendant's alibi.

Complement / Compliment: Complement means "to make complete," while compliment means "to praise."

> Bill's green sofa *complemented* his yellow drapes.
> Janet *complimented* Bill for his fine taste.

Correspond to / Correspond with: Correspond to means "in agreement with," while "correspond with" means "to exchange letters."

> The punishment does not *correspond to* the severity of the offense.
> Dana *corresponded with* many of the most desirable stars in Hollywood.

Emigrated / Immigrated

Emigrated means to leave one country for another.
> Jane's family *emigrated from* China to pursue a better life.

Immigrate means to establish permanent residence in a new country.
> My ancestors *immigrated to* America to attend college.

Flouting / Flaunting: Flout means "to scorn," while flaunt means "to show off."

> The angry boy *flouted* his parents' rules
> Grace wore sexy clothes to *flaunt* her voluptuous figure.

Lay / Lie

Lay means to place an object down.
> Please *lay* your coat on the bed.

Lie means to recline your body at rest.
> I will *lie* on the bed until my dizziness passes.

Leave / Let

Leave means depart.
>I will *leave* the party after they cut the cake.

Let means to allow.
>I will *let* Amy go to the party if she agrees to return by 6.

Raise / Rise

Raise means to elevate something.
>The stored *raised* it price on bread.

Rise means to get up.
>Sara *rises* at 6 am each morning.

Set / Sit

Set means to put something down.
>Bill *set* the plates on the table.

Sit means to take a seat.
>Bill will *sit* in Dad's seat at the table.

Speak to / with:

To *speak to* someone is to tell them something:
>We *spoke to* Jan about the new office hours.

To *speak with* someone is to discuss something with them.
>Sara *spoke with* Jan several weeks ago.

Wait for / wait on:

Wait for means to await, while wait on means to serve someone.

>Joe was *waiting for* Sara to call.
>The server *waited on* three other tables before ours.

Most Common Idiomatic Mistakes on the GRE™

Idiomatic mistakes occur when verbs are matched with the wrong prepositions. Before you take the GRE, review this list of common verbs, which we have matched with the CORRECT prepositions.

OF   Accuse of, Approve of, Consist of

WITH   Work with, Cover with

FOR   Apologize for, Blame for, Thank for, Vote for, Wait for, Substitute for, Excuse for, Forgive for, Pray For, Hope for

ABOUT   Worry about, Complain about, Forget about

TO   Respond to, Subscribe to, Contribute to, Object to

IN   Succeed in, Participate in, Excel in, Believe in

FROM   Prevent from, Prohibit from, Protect from, Recover from, Stop from, Escape from, Hide from, Distinguish from

AT   Stare at, Arrive at

ON / UPON   Count on, upon   Decide on, upon   Depend on, upon   Rely on, upon   Insist on, upon

FOR /WITH   Charge for, with   Provide for, with

MISCELLANEOUS

Care for, about
Discriminate against
Apply to, for
Differ from, with, over, about
Dream of, about
Agree to, with, on
Compare to, with
Abide by, in
Argue with, about

Appendix 7: Review of Math Topics for the GRE™

A. BASIC ARITHMETIC

Perfect squares include 1, 4, 9, 16, 25, 36, 49, 64, 81, 100
Perfect cubes include 1, 8, 27, 64 and 125

Commutative property: $x + y = y + x$
Associative property: $(x + y) + z = x + (y + z)$
Transitive property: If $x < y$ and $y < z$, then $x < z$

Like inequalities can be added: If $x < y$ and $w < z$, then $x + w < y + z$
Multiplying both sides of an inequality by a negative number reverses the inequality:
If $x > y$ and $c < 0$, then $cx < cy$

B. NUMBER PROPERTIES

1. Integers

Integers are whole numbers.. .-4,-3,-2,-1,0, 1,2,3,4,5.......
Positive integers are the numbers 1,2,3,4,5....
Zero is neither positive nor negative.
Negative integers are the numbers -1,-2,-3,-4,-5,-6,-7

Consecutive integers are written as x, $x+1$, $x+2$,....
Consecutive even or odd integers are written as x, $x+2$, $x+4$, $x+6$,.....

2. Non-integers

Non-integers are numbers that have a fractional part.
Examples of non-integers are t, 3.75, -1/2, 5/6 and π.

3. Multiplying/Dividing Signed Numbers

To multiply and/or divide positives and negatives, treat the numbers as usual and *attach a minus sign if there were originally an odd number of negatives.*

For example, to multiply -2, -4, and -6, first multiply the number parts:
$2 \times 4 \times 6 = 30$. Then go back and note that there were three negatives (an odd number), so the product is negative: $(-2) \times (-4) \times (-6) = -48$.

4. Order of Operations

Perform multiple operations in the following order:

   a.   Parentheses
   b.   Exponents
   c.   Multiplication and Division (left to right)
   d.   Addition and Subtraction (left to right)

5. Counting Consecutive Integers

To count consecutive integers, *subtract the smallest from the largest and add 1.* To count the integers from 18 through 56, subtract: 56 -18 = 38.   Then add 1: 38 + 1 = 39.

6. Absolute Value

The absolute value of any number is its distance from zero on the number line. The absolute value of a positive number is simply that number. To find the absolute value of a negative number, just drop the negative sign.

C. DIVISIBILITY

1. Factor/Multiple

The factors of integer x are the positive integers that divide into x with no remainder. The multiples of x are the integers that x divides into with no remainder.

For example, 6 is a factor of 18, and 48 is a multiple of 12. 12 is both a factor and a multiple of itself, since 12 X 1 = 12 and 12/1 = 12.

2. Prime Number

A prime number is a positive integer greater than 1, which has only two different positive factors, itself and 1.

For example, 7 is a prime number because the only positive factors of 7 are 1 and 7. If any other positive integer divides evenly into the integer, it isn't prime. For example, 12 is not a prime number.   2 is the only even prime.   2 is also the smallest prime number. 1 is not a prime number because it only has one positive factor: itself.

3. Prime Factorization

To find the prime factorization of an integer, just keep breaking it into factors until all the factors are prime.

Example: To find the prime factorization of 72, for example, you could begin by breaking it into 2 X 36 = 2 X 2 X 18 = 2 X 2 X 2 X 9 = 2 X 2 X 2 X 3 X 3.

4. Common Multiple

A common multiple is a number that is a multiple of two or more positive integers. For example, to find a common multiple for 12 and 15, you could just multiply: 12 X 15 = 180.

5. Least Common Multiple

To find the least common multiple, check out the positive multiples of the larger integer until you find one that is *also* a multiple of the smaller.

Example: To find the LCM of 12 and 15, begin by taking the multiples of 15. Our goal is to find the first one that is evenly divisible by 12. 15 is not divisible by 12; 30 is not, nor is 45.   But the *next* multiple of 15, which is 60, is divisible by 12, so it is the LCM.

6. Greatest Common Factor

To find the greatest common factor, break down both integers into their prime factorizations and multiply all of the prime factors they have in common.

Example: 36 = 2 X 2 X 3 X 3, and 64 = 2 X 2 X 2 X 2 X 2 X 2.
What they have in common are two 2s, so the GCF is 2 X 2 = 4.

7. Even/Odd

To predict whether a sum, difference, or product will be even or odd, just take simple numbers such as 1 and 2 and see what happens. Although there are rules, such as *odd times even is even*, there is no need to memorize them. What happens with one set of numbers is generally what will happen with all similar sets.

8. Divisibility Rules:

An integer is divisible by 2 (even) if the *last digit* is even.
An integer is divisible by 4 if the last *two digits* form a multiple of 4.
An integer is divisible by 3 if the *sum of its digits* is divisible by 3.
An integer is divisible by 9 if the *sum of its digits* is divisible by 9.
An integer is divisible by 5 if the *last digit* is 5 or 0.
An integer is divisible by 10 if the *last digit* is 0.

9. Remainders

The remainder is the whole number that is left over after division.   237 is 2 more than 235, which is a multiple of 5, so when 237 is divided by 5, the remainder will be 2.

D. FRACTIONS AND DECIMALS

1. Reducing Fractions

To reduce a fraction to lowest terms, factor out and cancel all factors the numerator and denominator have in common.

18/52 = (2 X 9)/(2 x 26) = 9/26

2. Adding/Subtracting Fractions

To add or subtract fractions, first find a common denominator, then add or subtract the numerators. To find a common denominator, find the LCM of the denominators and multiply the fractions accordingly:

 2/15 + 3/10 = 4/30 + 9/30 = (4 + 9)/30 = 13/30

3. Multiplying Fractions

To multiply fractions, multiply the numerators and multiply the denominators.

5/4 x 7/11 = (5 x 7)/(4 x 11) = 35/44

4. Dividing Fractions

To divide fractions, invert the second one and multiply.

(1/2) / (3/7) = (1/2) x (7/3) = 7/6

5. Improper Fractions and Mixed Numbers

Fractions that have an absolute value > 1 can be written either as the sum of an integer and a fraction (a mixed number) or as a single fraction (an improper fraction).

For example, 9- 2/5 is a mixed number that can be thought of as 9 + 2/5 and rewritten as the improper fraction 47/5.

6. Reciprocal

To find the reciprocal of a number, reverse the numerator and the denominator.

Example: The reciprocal of 1/2 is 2/1 or 2. The reciprocal of 2/5 is 5/2.

The product of reciprocals is always 1.

7. Comparing Fractions

a) One way to compare fractions is to re-express them with a common denominator.

Example. Compare 3/4 and 5/9.   3/4 = 27/36, while 5/9 = 20/36   Hence, 3/4 is larger than 5/9

b) Another way to compare fractions is to convert them both to decimals.

Example: 3/4 converts to .75, and 5/9 converts to approximately .555.

8. Converting Fractions & Decimals

To convert a fraction to a decimal, divide the bottom into the top. To convert 5/6, divide 6 into 5, yielding 0.833.

To convert a decimal to a fraction, set the decimal over 1 and *multiply the numerator and denominator by ten raised to the number of digits to the right of the decimal point*.

Example: to convert 0.375 to a fraction, you would multiply (375/1) x (1000/1000). Then simplify, yielding: 375/1000 = (15 x 25)/(40 x 25) = (3 x 5) / (8 x 5) = 3/8

9. Identifying the Parts and the Whole

The key to solving most word problems with fractions and percentages is to identify the part and the whole. Usually you'll find the **part** associated with the verb *is/are* and the **whole** associated with the word *of*.

Example: In the sentence, "Half of the girls are Freshmen," the whole is the girls and the part is the Freshmen.

E. PERCENT

1. Percent Formula: Part = Percent X Whole

Example: What is 32% of 25?   Setup: Part = .32 X 25

Example: 15 is 12% of what number?   Setup: 15 = .12 X Whole

Example: 25 is what percent of 7?   Setup: 25 = Percent X 7

2. Percent Increase and Decrease

To increase a number by a percent, *add the percent to 100 percent*, convert to a decimal, and multiply.   To increase 60 by 25 percent, add 25 percent to 100 percent, convert 125 percent to 1.25, and multiply by 60.   1.25 X 60 = 75.

3. Finding the Original Whole

To find the original whole before a percent increase or decrease, set up an equation. Think of the result of a 17 percent increase over x as 1.17x.

Example: After a 75 percent increase, the population was 5,879. What was the population before the increase? Setup: 1.07x = 5,879

4. Combined Percent Increase and Decrease

To determine the combined effect of multiple percent increases and/or decreases, start with 100 and then combine.

Example: A price went up 12 percent one year, and the new price went up 24 percent the next year. What was the combined percent increase?

Setup: First year: 100 + (12 percent of 100) =112.
Second year: 112 + (24 percent of 112) = 139.

That equals a combined increase of 39 percent.

F. RATIOS, PROPORTIONS, AND RATES

1. Definitions.

A **ratio** can be used to compare two quantities (if a class contains 20 students, of which 7 are male and 13 are female, then the ratio 7/20 compares the number of *male students* in the class to the *total number* of students).

Ratios can be presented in one of three ways (in each case below, the expression reads "3 to 5:"

3 to 5   3:5   3/5

A **proportion** is a mathematical statement in which two ratios are equal:

10/25 = 2/5   0.050/0.50 = 1/10   80/4 = 20/1

By definition, for the ratio A/B = C/D, AD = BC

2. Setting up a Ratio

To find a ratio, put the number associated with the word *of* in the nominator and the quantity associated with the word *to* in the denominator. Then reduce.

Example: The ratio of 15 cakes to 12 candies is 15/12, which reduces to 5/4.

3. Part-to-Part Ratios and Part-to-Whole Ratios

If the parts add up to the whole, a part-to-part ratio can be turned into two part-to-whole ratios by putting each number in the original ratio over the sum of the numbers.

Example: If the ratio of cats to dogs is 1 to 5, then the cat-to-whole ratio is 1 / (1 + 5) = 1/6 and the dog-to-whole ratio is 5 / (1 + 5) = 5/6. In other words, 5/6 of the animals are dogs.

4. Using Ratios to Solve Rate Problems

Example: If snow is falling at the rate of one foot every four hours, how many inches of snow will fall in seven hours?

$$\frac{1 \text{ foot}}{4 \text{ hours}} = \frac{x \text{ inches}}{7 \text{ hours}}$$

Next, make the units the same:

$$\frac{12 \text{ inches}}{4 \text{ hours}} = \frac{x \text{ inches}}{7 \text{ hours}}$$

Finally, solve for x: 4x= 12 x 7, so x= 21 inches of snow will fall in 7 hours

5. Average Rate

The average rate or speed = Total distance / Total time

6. Common Formulas for Word Problems:

a) *Distance = Rate x Time*

Example: Two cars leave Milwaukee at the same time traveling in opposite directions. One car travels at 60 mph and the other travels at 50 mph. In how many hours will they be 880 miles apart?

Let R1 be the rate of the first car; let R2 be the rate of the second car
Let T1 be the time of the first car; let T2 be the time of the second car

The distance the first car travels is R1 x T1 and the distance the second car travels is R2 x T2

R1 T1 + R2 T2 = 880. We also know that T1 = T2. Our new equation is:60T + 50T = 880
T = 8   Hence, it will take 8 hours for the cars to be 880 miles apart.

b) *Work = Rate x Time*

Example: If Jasmine can sew a dress alone in 6 days and Amy can sew the same dress in 8 days, how long will it take them to sew the dress if they both work on it?

Let x be the number of hours if they work together.

	Jasmine	Amy	Together
Hours to sew	6	8	x
Part done in one day	1	1	1

1/6 + 1/8 = 1/x. Solving for x, we get 3 3/7 days

c) *Interest = Principal Amount x Rate x Time*

Example: If Michelle has $6,700 in a bank that pays 4% simple interest for three years, how much interest will she earn in three years? (Assume no compounding).

Interest = Principal Amount x Rate x Time = (6700)(0.04)(3) = $804

G. MEAN, MEDIAN AND MODE

1. Average or Arithmetic Mean

To find the average of a set of numbers, add them up and divide by the number of numbers.

Average = Sum of the terms / The number of items

Example: To find the average of the five numbers 12, 15, 23, 40, and 40, first add them:
12 + 15 + 23 + 40 + 40 = 130. Then divide the sum by 5: 130 / 5 = 26.

2. Using the Average to Find the Sum

Sum = (Average) X (Number of terms)

Example: If the average of ten numbers is 60, then they add up to 10 X 60, or 600.

3. Finding a Missing Number

To find a missing number when you are given the average, use the sum.

Example: If the average of four numbers is 7, then the sum of those four numbers is 4 X 7, or 28.
Suppose that three of the numbers are 3, 5, and 8. These three numbers add up to 16 of that 28, which leaves 12 for the fourth number.

4. Median

The median of a set of numbers is the value that falls in the middle of the set.

Example: If you have five test scores - 88, 86, 57, 94, and 73 - you must first list the scores in increasing or decreasing order: 57, 73, 86, 88, 94.

The median is the middle number, or 86. If there is an even number of values in a set (six test scores, for instance), simply take the average of the two middle numbers.

5. Mode

The mode of a set of numbers is the value that appears most often.

Example: If your test scores were 88, 57, 68, 85,99, 93, 93, 84, and 81, the mode of the scores would be 93 because it appears more often than any other score.

If there is a tie for the most common value in a set, the set has more than one mode (and is called bi-modal).

6. Standard Deviation

The Standard Deviation is a complex statistical measure, but for the test you mainly need to know that the it is the measure of how spread out a group of numbers are.

For example, the numbers {0, 10, 20} have a Standard Deviation of about 8.17 while the numbers {9, 10, 11} have a Standard Deviation of about 0.82. Both have an average of 10, but because the first group was more "spread out" it had a higher Standard Deviation.

H. POSSIBILITY AND PROBABILITY

1. Number of Possibilities

The fundamental counting principle: If there are m ways one event can happen and n ways a second event can happen, then there are m x n ways for the two events to happen.

Example: With five sweaters and six skirts, you can put together 5 X 6 = 30 different outfits.

2. Probability

Probability   =   Favorable outcomes / Total possible outcomes

For example, if you have 12 ties in a drawer and 8 of them are blue, the probability of picking a blue tie at random is 8/12 = 2/3. This probability can also be expressed as .67 or 67 percent.

3. Conditional Probability

A conditional probability is the probability that one event occurs given that a second event occurred. The probability of two separate events occurring is the *product* of the probability of the first event occurring and the conditional probability of the second event occurring (given that the first event occurred).

Example: If you have 3 red candies and 4 orange candies in a bag, the probability of withdrawing an orange candy is 4/7 (since we have 4 orange candies out of a total of 7 candies).

If an orange candy is withdrawn and not replaced, then the probability of withdrawing another orange candy is 3/6 (since we now have 3 orange candies and a total of 6 candies left).

So the probability of withdrawing two orange candies in a row is: 4/7 x 3/6 = 12/42 = 2/7

4. Permutations

Sometimes, a word problem will ask us to determine the number of ways we can arrange elements sequentially, such as people in a line or items on a shelf. The solution is simply a **factorial**: the number of possibilities for the first item times the number of possibilities for the second times the number of possibilities for the third item, etc.

Example: How many different ways can we arrange six different books on a shelf?

Solution: The number of possibilities will be 6! = 6 x 5 x 4 x 3 x 2 x 1 = **720 possible ways**.

Other times, we will be asked to determine the number of ways to arrange a smaller group that is being drawn from a larger group. In this case, we must use the mathematical formula for permutations:

$$P(n,r) = \frac{n!}{(n-r)!}.$$

Where **n** = the number of items in the larger group and **r** = the number of items we are choosing

Example: Six artists submit their paintings in a competitive art show. The artists who win the first, second and third place prizes will each receive a cash award. How many possible outcomes are there for the first, second, and third place prizes?

Solution: 6! / (6-3)! = 6! / 3! = 6 x 5 x 4 = **120 possible outcomes**.

An important point about permutations – the order MATTERS. In the example above, it matters which artist won first, second, and third place; we cannot simply move their positions within the group. Hence, *every time we move an artist to a new position, it constitutes a new arrangement.*

5. Combinations

Sometimes, a word problem will ask us to consider different combinations of items within a larger group. If the order or arrangement of the items in the smaller group does NOT matter, then we can simply calculate the number of *possible* combinations. Our formula is:

$$^nC_k = \binom{n}{k} = \frac{n!}{k!(n-k)!}.$$

Where **n** = the number of items in the larger group and **k** = the number of items we are choosing

Example: How many different ways can we choose five pizza toppings from a selection of eight?

Solution: The order of the toppings does not matter. Thus, we can use the formula for combinations to solve it:

8C5 = 8! / [5!(8 – 5)!] = 8! / 5! x 3! = (8 x 7 x 6 x 5!) / (8 x 7 x 6 x 5!) / (5! x 3 x 2 x 1) = 56 different ways

I. SERIES AND SEQUENCES

1. Series

A series is a progression of numbers that are arranged according to a specific design.

The easiest ones are *arithmetic progressions*, such as 3, 5, 7, 9,….. in which each number is two digits greater than the previous one in the series. Likewise, series can include examples such as 2, 4, 16, 256, etc., in which the each number is the perfect square of the preceding number.

2. Arithmetic Sequence

Standardized tests often ask students to calculate the *nth* term in an arithmetic sequence – or the sum of a particular set of consecutive integers. For these questions, it's extremely helpful to use the relevant algebraic formulas:

Sum = Number of Items (First Item + Last or Desired Item) / 2

Example: What is the sum of the first 15 positive integers?

Sum = 15(1 + 15)/2 = (15)(16)/2 = 120

For an arithmetic sequence in which the first term is **A** and the difference between the terms is **D**, the *nth* term is: **An = A1 + (n − 1)D**

Example: What is the eighth even positive integer? A8 = 2 + (8 − 1)2 = 2 + 14 = 16.

3.Items in a Consecutive Series

To determine the number of items in a consecutive set, **subtract the endpoints and add 1.**

Example: A bookkeeper has a stack of invoices numbered 00236 through 00435. How many invoices were in the stack?

Solution: 00435 - 00236 + 1 = 200. There were 200 invoices in the stack. Choice C is correct.

J. EXPONENTS AND RADICALS

1. Multiplying and Dividing Powers

To multiply powers with the same base, add the exponents and keep the same base:

$$b^3 \ x \ b^4 = \ b^{3+4} \ = \ b^7$$

To divide powers with the same base, subtract the exponents and keep the same base:

$$b^{12} / b^8 \ = \ b^{12-8} \ = b^4$$

2. Raising Powers to Powers

To raise a power to a power, multiply the exponents:

$$(x^3)^5 \ = \ x^{3x5} \ = \ x^{15}$$

3. Negative Powers

A number raised to a negative exponent is simply the reciprocal of that number raised to the corresponding positive exponent.

$$2^{-3} = 1/2^3 = 1/8$$

4. Simplifying Square Roots

To simplify a square root, factor out the perfect squares under the radical, un-square them and put the result in front: $\sqrt{12} = \sqrt{4X3} = \sqrt{4} \ X \ \sqrt{3} \ = 2\sqrt{3}$

5. Adding and Subtracting Roots

You can add or subtract radical expressions when the part under the radical signs is the same:

$$2\sqrt{7} + 3\sqrt{7} = 5\sqrt{7}$$

Don't try to add or subtract when the radicals are different. You cannot simplify expressions like:

$2 \sqrt{3} + 3 \sqrt{5}$

6. Multiplying and Dividing Roots

The product of square roots is equal to the square root of the product:

$\sqrt{2} \times \sqrt{3} = \sqrt{(2 \times 3)} = \sqrt{6}$

The quotient of square roots is equal to the square root of the quotient:

$\sqrt{8} / \sqrt{2} = \sqrt{8/4} = \sqrt{2}$

K. ALGEBRAIC EXPRESSIONS

1. Evaluating an Expression

To evaluate an algebraic expression, plug in the given values for the unknowns and calculate according to the rules for the order of operations.

Example: To find the value of $x^2 + 3x - 1$ when $x = -2$, plug in -2 for x:
$(-2)(-2) + 3(-2) - 1 = 4 - 6 - 1 = -3$.

2. Adding and Subtracting Monomials

To combine like terms, keep the variable unchanged while adding or subtracting the coefficients: $9a + 4a = (9 + 4)a = 13a$

3. Adding and Subtracting Polynomials

To add or subtract polynomials, combine like terms.

$(3x^2 + 5x - 7) - (x^2 + 12) = (3x^2 - x^2) + 5x + (-7 - 12) = 2x^2 + 5x - 19$

4. Multiplying Monomials

To multiply monomials, multiply the coefficients and the variables separately:

$2a \times 3a = (2 \times 3)(a \times a) = 6a^2$

5. Multiplying Binomials

To multiply binomials such as $(x + 4) (x + 3)$, use the following order:

First multiply the first terms: x times $x = x^2$
Next multiply the outer terms: x times 4 = 4x.
Then multiply the inner terms: 3 times x = 3x.
Last, multiply the last terms: 3 times 4 = 12.

Then, add and combine like terms: $x^2 + 4x + 3x + 12 = x^2 + 7x + 12$

6. Multiplying Other Polynomials

To multiply polynomials with more than two terms, make sure you multiply each term in the first polynomial by each term in the second.

$(x^2 + 3x + 4)$ times $(x + 5) =$

$x^2 \ (x + 5) + 3x \ (x + 5) + 4 \ (x + 5) =$

$x^3 + 5x^2 + 3x^2 + 15x + 4x + 20 =$

$x^3 + 8x^2 + 19x + 20$

After multiplying two polynomials together, the number of terms in your expression before simplifying should equal the number of terms in one polynomial multiplied by the number of terms in the second. In the example above, you should have 3 X 2 = 6 terms in the product before you simplify like terms.

L. FACTORING ALGEBRAIC EXPRESSIONS

1. Factoring the Difference of Squares

One of the test makers' favorite factorable expressions is the difference of squares.

$a^2 - b^2 = (a -b) (a + b) = a^2 - 9$, which factors to $(a - 3)(a + 3)$.

2. Factoring the Square of a Binomial

Learn to recognize polynomials that are squares of binomials:

$a^2 + 2ab + b = (a + b)^2$

$a^2 - 2ab + b = (a - b)^2$

Examples: $4x^2 + 12x + 9$ factors to $(2x + 3)^2$ and $n^2 - 10n + 25$ factors to $(n -5)^2.$

3. Simplifying an Algebraic Fraction

Simplifying an algebraic fraction is a lot like simplifying a numerical fraction: find factors that are common to the numerator and denominator and cancel them.

Example: Take the rather cumbersome expression:

$(a^2 + 7a + 12)/(a^2 - 9) = \{(a + 3) (a + 4)\} / \{(a + 3)(a - 3)\}$

Thus, we can cancel out the identical expressions $(a + 3)$ in the numerator and denominator, which leaves us with $(a + 4) (a - 3)$.

M. SOLVING EQUATIONS

1. Solving a Linear Equation

To solve an equation, isolate the variable. For the equation: $4x -12 = -3x + 9$, first combine the terms that contain an x by adding 3x to both sides: $7x -12 = 9$. Then add 12 to both sides: $7x = 21$. Then divide both sides by 7: $x = 3$.

2. Solving "In Terms Of Another Variable"

To solve an equation for one variable in terms of another, *isolate one variable on one side of the equation,* which will leave an expression that contains the other variable on the other side of the equation.

Example: To solve the equation $6x - 9y = 10x + 3y$ for x in terms of y, isolate x:

$6x - 9y = 10x + 3y$
$6x = 10x + 12y$
$-4x = 12y$
$x = -3y$

3. Solving a Quadratic Equation

To solve a quadratic equation, follow these steps:

a) Arrange the equation in the form: "$ax^2 + bx + c = 0$"
b) Factor the left side
c) Set each factor equal to 0 separately to get the two solutions.

To solve $x^2 + 12 = 7x$, first rewrite it as $x^2 - 7x + 12 = 0$ Then factor the left side:
$(x - 3)(x - 4) = 0$
$x - 3 = 0$ or $x - 4 = 0$
$X = 3$ or 4

4. Solving a System of Equations

You can solve for two variables *only* if you have two distinct equations. Combine the equations to cancel out one of the variables.

Example: Our equations are: $x + y = 100$ and $3x + y = 150$

In this scenario, we can easily rearrange the first equation to read $y = 100 - x$. We can then substitute this value for y in equation two, and solve for x. When we do, we get:

$3x + (100 - x) = 150$
$3x + 100 - x = 150$
$2x = 50$
$x = 25$

Now, we can plug $x = 25$ into either equation to solve for y. $y = 75$.

5. Solving an Inequality

To solve an inequality, isolate the variable. Just remember that when you multiply or divide both sides by a negative number, you must reverse the sign.

Example: To solve $-5x + 7 < -3$, subtract 7 from both sides to get: $-5x < -10$. Now divide both sides by -5, remembering to reverse the sign: $x > 2$.

N. WORD PROBLEMS

Word problems account for a significant number of the questions on the exam. Although many students are intimidated by them, word problems actually test the *same* concepts as other questions (algebra, math, geometry), but require you to translate the situation from ordinary language into mathematical terms.

Example: A typical algebra problem might have the equation $3b = f - 4$.

In a word problem, this would translate into: If Beth had three times as many candy bars, she would have four candy bars less than Francesca.

To translate from words into algebra, look for the key words and phrases that you must turn into algebraic expressions. Here are the most typical conversions:

Concept	Symbol	Words	Example	Translation
Equality	=	is equals is the same as	2 plus 3 is 5 c minus 2 equals 5	$2 + 3 = 5$ $c - 2 = 5$
Addition	+	plus add increase	x plus z equals n J adds x to 13 n is increased by 3%	$x + z = n$ $x + 13 = J$ $n + 0.03n$
Subtraction	-	minus difference	x minus y	$x - y$
Multiplication	x	times product of	x is 125% of y	$x = 125\%y$
Division	/	quotient	x divided by y is 4	$x/y = 4$

Here are several examples of converting English into algebra:

a) Beth gets 4 dollars more than twice Amy's salary: $B = 4 + 2A$

b) A quarter of the sum of a and b is 4 less than a: $0.25(a + b) = a - 4$

c) If $200 is taken from Jake's salary, then the combined salaries of Jake and Kate will be double what Jake's salary would be if it was increased by one third of itself: $J - 200 + K = 2 (J + J/3)$

d) Tara's age is 5 years less than twice Jade's age and the sum of their ages is 16:
(J = Jade's age). $(2J - 5) + J = 16$

The most difficult part of a word problem is correctly translating the original words into an algebraic equation. Here are our best tips for approaching word problems:

1) First, choose a variable to stand for the least unknown quantity and then write the other unknown quantities in terms of that variable.

2) Second, write an equation based on the situation given. Most test problems pivot on two quantities being equal.

3) Solve the equation and interpret the result.

Example: If three less than eleven times a whole number is equal to 140, what is the number?

In this case, we will let x = the whole number we are trying to find. Once we define our variable, the problem easily converts to a simple equation:
$11x - 3 = 140$
$11x = 143$
$x = 13$

166

Example: When Sara and Claire got dressed for the prom, they checked out each other's makeup collections. If Sara has six more than three times number of tubes of lipstick than Claire has, and Claire has eighteen tubes of lipstick, how many tubes does Sara have?

We can write a simple equation to calculate the answer. First let's define our unknown, x, as the number of tubes of lipstick that Sara owns. According to the problem, $x = 3(18) + 6 = 60$ tubes of lipstick.

O. COORDINATE GEOMETRY

1. Plotting a Point on the xy Plane

Points in the xy-plane are represented by two numbers called coordinates:

a) The first number in the pair is the *x-coordinate,* which is the horizontal distance of the point from the origin, which is point (0,0). Points with positive x-coordinates are to the right of the y-axis. Points with negative x-coordinates are to the left of the y-axis.

b) The second number is the *y-coordinate*, which is the vertical distance from the origin.   Points with positive y- coordinates are above the x-axis. Points with negative y-coordinates are below the x-axis.

c) A point is represented by the ordered pair (x, y), in which x is called the *abscissa* and y is called the *ordinate.*

2. Finding the Midpoint of a Line

Example: A line segment is drawn from the point (3, 5) to the point (9, 13). What are the coordinates of the midpoint of this line segment?

Solution: Add the x values and divide by two. (3 + 9) / 2 = 6. Then, add the y values and divide by two (5 + 13) / 2 = 9.   Thus, the coordinates of the midpoint of the line are (6, 9).

3. Using Two Points to Find the Slope

Slope = Change in y = Rise
Change in x   Run

The slope of the line that contains the points A (2, 3) and B (0, -1) is:

$(y_2 - y_1) / (x_2 - x_1) = (-1 - 3) / (0 - 2) = -4 / -2 = 2$

4. Using an Equation to Find the Slope

To find the slope *of* a line from an equation, put the equation into the **slope-intercept** form:
$y = mx + b$

The slope is m and the y-intercept is b.   To find the slope of the equation $3x + 2y = 4$, rearrange it to get $y = -3/2 x + 4$. The slope is   -3/4

5. Using an Equation to Find an Intercept

To find the **y-intercept**, either:

a) put the equation into $y = mx + b$ (slope-intercept) form - b is the y-intercept
b) plug x = 0 into the equation and solve for *y.*

To find the **x-intercept**, plug $y = 0$ into the equation and solve for *x*.

P. LINES AND ANGLES

1. Intersecting Lines

When two lines intersect, four angles are formed. **Adjacent angles are supplementary and vertical angles are equal.**

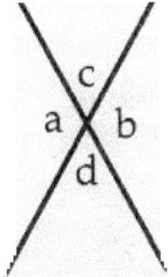

a = b, and c = d

Vertical Angles: those opposite each other; are always equal

Straight Angles: has its sides lying along a straight line; is always equal to 180 degrees

Adjacent Angles: two angles are adjacent if they share the same vertex and a common side, but no angle is inside another angle.

Supplementary Angles: if the sum of two angles is a straight line (180 degrees), the two angles are supplementary and each angle is the supplement of the other

Right Angles: if two supplementary angles are equal, they are both right angles. A right angle is half of a straight line and measures exactly 90 degrees.

Complementary Angles: two angles whose sum is 90 degrees
Acute Angles: those whose measure is less than 90 degrees

Obtuse Angles: those whose measure is greater than 90 degrees but less than 180 degrees

Q. TRIANGLES

1. Interior Angles of a Triangle

The three interior angles of any triangle add up to 180 degrees

<u>Example</u>: In triangle XYZ, angle Y is twice angle X and angle Z is 40 degrees more than angle Y. How many degrees are in the three angles?

Solution: Knowing that the three angles must total 180 degrees, solve this using an algebraic equation. Let x = angle X, 2x = angle Y, and 2x + 40 = angle Z:

$x + 2x + (2x + 40) = 180$. Solving for X, we find that:

Angle X = 28 degrees   Angle Y = 56 degrees   Angle Z = 96 degrees

2. Similar Triangles

Similar triangles have the same shape; corresponding angles are equal and corresponding sides are proportional.

3. Area of a Triangle = 1/2 (Base) (Height)

The height is the perpendicular distance between the side that is chosen as the base and the opposite vertex.

Example: If a triangle of base 6 has the same area as a circle of radius 6, what is the altitude of the triangle?

Solution: The area of the circle is $\pi r^2 = \pi(6)(6) = 36\pi$. In the triangle, the area = 1/2 (Base) (Height). We will let x = the height. Thus, for this triangle, 1/2 (6)x = 36 π. x = 12 π. Choice C is correct.

4. Triangle Inequality Theorem

The length of one side of a triangle must be **greater than the difference and less than the sum of** the lengths of the other two sides.

Example: If a problem states that the length of one side of a triangle is 3 and the length of another side is 7, then the length of the third side must be greater than 7 -3 = 4 and less than 7 + 3 = 10.

5. Isosceles Triangles

An isosceles triangle is a triangle that has **two equal sides.** Not only are two sides equal, but the angles opposite the equal sides, called base angles, are also equal.

Example: The vertex angle of an isosceles triangle is G degrees. How many degrees are there in one of the base angles?

Solution: Since the vertex angle = G, the sum of the other two angles = 180 – G. Each base angle therefore contains 1/2(180 – G) degrees.

6. Equilateral Triangles

In equilateral triangles, **all three sides (and all three angles) are equal.** All three angles in an equilateral triangle measure 60 degrees, regardless of the lengths of sides.

R. RIGHT TRIANGLES

By definition, a right triangle contains a 90 degree angle.

1. Pythagorean Theorem

For all right triangles: $(\text{leg})^2 + (\text{1eg})^2 = (\text{hypotenuse})^2$

Example: If ABC is a right triangle with a right angle at B, and if AB = 6 and BC = 8, what is the length of AC?

Solution: Use the Pythagorean theorem, $AB^2 + BC^2 = AC^2$ (6)(6) + (8)(8) = 100   AC = 10

2. The 3-4-5 Triangle

If a right triangle's leg-to-leg ratio is 3:4, or if the leg-to-hypotenuse ratio is 3:5 or 4:5, it's a 3-4-5 triangle. In this case, we don't need to use the Pythagorean theorem to find the third side. Just figure out what multiple of 3-4-5 it is.

3. 5-12-13 Triangle

If a right triangle's leg-to-leg ratio is 5:12, or if the leg-to-hypotenuse ratio is 5:13 or 12:13, then it's a 5-12-13 triangle. In this case, we don't need to use the Pythagorean theorem to find the third side. Just figure out what multiple of 5-12-13 it is.

Example: What is the area of a right triangle with sides 5, 12 and 13?

Solution: The triangle has a hypotenuse of 13 and legs of 12 and 5. Since the legs are perpendicular to each other, we can use one as the base and the other as the height of the triangle. Area = 1/2 bh = 1/2 (12)(5) = 30

4. 30-60-90 Triangle

The sides of a 30-60-90 triangle are in a ratio of $x : x\sqrt{3} : 2x$. We don't need to use the Pythagorean theorem.

5. 45-45-90 Triangle

The sides of a 45-45-90 triangle are in a ratio of $x : x : x\sqrt{2}$

If one leg is 3, then the other leg is also 3, and the hypotenuse is equal to a leg times the square root of two, or 3 times the square root of two.

S. OTHER POLYGONS

1. Characteristics of a Rectangle

A rectangle is a four-sided figure with four right angles. Opposite sides are equal. The diagonals are also equal.

2. Area of a Rectangle   Area of Rectangle = Length X Width

3. Characteristics of a Parallelogram

A parallelogram has two pairs of parallel sides. Additionally, both opposite sides and opposite angles are equal. Further, the sum of all consecutive angles is 180 degrees.

Example: In parallelogram ABCD, angle A is four times angle B. What is the measure in degrees of angle A?

Solution: The consecutive angles of a parallelogram are supplementary, so:
x + 4x = 180, x = 36. Thus, angle A is 4(36) = 144 degrees

170

4. Area of a Parallelogram   Area of Parallelogram = Base X Height

5. Characteristics of a Square

A square is a **rectangle with four equal** sides. Thus, the perimeter of a square is equal to four times the length of one side.

6. Area of a Square   Area of Square = Side Length x Side Length

Example: Square 1 has a side length of 3. Square 2 has a side length of 9. What is the ratio of their areas?
Solution: The area of Square 1 is (3)(3) = 9. The area of Square 2 = (9)(9) = 81. The ratio of 9 to 81 is 1:9.

Example: Find the area (in square feet) of a square whose diagonal is 12 feet.

Solution: Knowing the square is actually 2 triangles that share the same hypotenuse (the diagonal), we can use the Pythagorean theorem to solve for the length of a side.

$s^2 + s^2 = 12^2$
$2s^2 = 144$
$s^2 = 72$
Side length = 8.485 feet. Therefore, the area of the square = 72.

T. CIRCLES

1. Characteristics of Circles

Circles are closed plane curves with all points on the curve equally distant from a fixed point called the center.

A radius of a circle is a line segment from the center to any point on the circle. All radii of a circle are equal.

A chord is a line segment whose endpoints are on the circle.

A diameter of a circle is a chord that passes through the center of the circle. The diameter of a circle is twice its radius and the longest distance between two points on the circle.

An arc is a portion of a circle, usually measured in degrees.
> The entire circle is 360 degrees
> A semicircle (half a circle) is 180 degrees
> A quarter of a circle is an arc of 90 degrees

A central angle is an angle whose vertex is the center of the circle and whose sides are radii of the circle. A central angle is equal in measure to its arc.

An inscribed angle is an angle whose vertex is on the circle and whose sides are chords of the circle. An inscribed angle is equal in measure to one-half its arc.

2. Circumference of a Circle: $2 \pi r$

Example: if the radius of a circle is 3, and so the circumference is $2 \times \pi \times 3 = 6 \pi$.

3. Length of an Arc

An arc is a portion of the circumference of a circle. If n is the degree measure of the arc's central angle, then the formula is: **Length of an Arc** = $(n/360)(2\pi r)$

<u>Example</u>: A circle has a radius of 5. The measure of the central angle is 72°. The arc length is 72/360 or 1/5 of the circumference: $(72/360)(2\pi)(5) = (1/5)(10\pi) = 2\pi$

4. Area of a Circle   Area of a Circle = πr^2

<u>Example</u>: What is the radius of the circle that passes through the point (10, 8) and has its center at (2, 2)?

Solution: This problem gives us two pieces of information about the circle – its center coordinates (2, 2) and a point on its circumference (10, 8). We can use the distance formula to find the radius of the circle:

Radius = $\sqrt{\{(10-2)(10-2) + (8-2)(8-2)\}}$
Radius = $\sqrt{\{(8)(8)+(6)(6)\}} = \sqrt{(64+36)} = \sqrt{100} = 10$
Thus, the radius of the circle is 10.

<u>Example</u>: If the diameter of a circle increases by 50%, by what percent will the area of the circle increase?

Solution: The area of the circle = πr^2. If the diameter is 4, the radius is 2 and the area is 4π. If we increase the diameter by 50% to 6, the new radius is 3 and the new area is 9π. The percent increase is (9 - 4)/4 = 5/4, or 125%.

To verify that this answer is correct, let's try another set of numbers. If the diameter is 10, the radius is 5 and the area is 25π. If we increase the diameter by 50% to 15, the new radius is 7.5 and the new area is 56.25π. The percent increase is (56.25 - 25)/25 = 5/4, or 125%.

5. Area of a Sector

A sector is a piece of the area of a circle. If n is the degree measure of the sector's central angle, then the formula is: Area of a Sector = $(n/360)(\pi)(r)(r)$

U. SOLIDS

1. Surface Area of a Rectangular Solid

The surface of a rectangular solid consists of three pairs of identical faces. To find the surface area, add the area of each face. If the length is l, the width is w, and the height is h, the formula is: Surface Area = *2lw + 2wh + 2lh*

<u>Example</u>: a rectangular solid has a length of 7, a width of 3 and a height of 4. Its surface area is 2(7)(3) + 2 (3)(4) + 2 (7)(4) = 42 + 24 + 56 = 122

2. Volume of a Rectangular Solid   = Length x Width x Height

A **cube** is a rectangular solid with length, width, and height that are all equal. If a is the length of an edge of a cube, the volume formula is: (a)(a)(a)

Example: For a cube with a side length of 2, the volume is (2)(2)(2) = 8.

Example: If the surface area of a cube is 486 square feet, how many cubic feet are there in the volume of the cube?

Solution: The surface area of the cube - 486 square feet - is composed of 6 equal sides. Thus, $486 = 6x^2$, where x= a side of the cube. $x^2 = 81$, or x = 9. The volume of the cube is $9^3 = 729$ cubic feet.

Example: Find the edge (in cm) of a cube whose volume is equal to the volume of a rectangular solid that is 8 cm by 18 cm by 96 cm.

Solution: The volume of the rectangular solid is Length x Width x Height = 8 x 18 x 96 = 13,824
The volume of the cube = 13,824 = (Side length)^3 Side length = 24.

3. Volume of a Cylinder = π x r^2 x Height

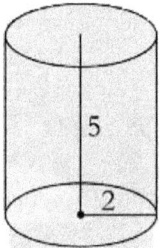

In the cylinder above, r = 2 and h = 5, so   Volume = π (2)(2)(5) = 20 π

Example: A cylindrical bucket has a diameter of 12 inches and a height of 14 inches. How many gallons will it hold of a liquid with a density of 84 cubic inches per gallon? (Use π = 3.1416)

Solution: The problem is asking us to determine the capacity, or volume, of a cylinder.   To do so, we can simply use the formula:

Volume = $\pi r^2 h$ = (3.1416)(6)(6)(14) = 1,583.37 cubic inches. To convert our answer to gallons, we must divide by 84: 1,583.37 cubic inches/84 cubic inches per gallon = 18.85 gallons.